James,

See you on Higher Ground

HANDSHAKE

What the Great Do That Others Don't

By Chris Sonksen

Published in Corona, California, by Celera Publishing.

Celera books may be purchased in bulk for educational, business, church, or sales promotional use. For information, please email info@celeragroup.org or visit us at www.celeragroup.org

Sonksen, Chris, 1968-

Handshake: What the Great Do that Others Don't

First Edition / Chris Sonksen

Includes Bibliographical References.

ISBN 10 digit 1-888741-28-7 (Hardcover)

1. Leadership 2. Personal Development 3. Motivational 4.Organization

This book is dedicated to Frank Colapinto.
Your handshake changed my life.

CONTENTS

1

THE CHOICE OF CONFIDENCE
Frank Colapinto

I was fifteen years old when I got my first real job. I was hired to clean office buildings at night for a company called Brown's Janitorial. Not the best job in the world, but for me, it beat working fast food. We started at 6:00 pm each night and finished around 11:00 pm. At times this was a difficult schedule considering I was only a sophomore in high school. But I had a strong work ethic, something I learned from my parents. I did what I needed to do.

I did not drive (or at least legally), so they would drop me off at one office building while they worked at another building across town. The duties were fairly simple: vacuum, empty trash, wipe desks and clean bathrooms. One of my assignments was a medium size office for a manufacturing company called "Design Gifts." This company designed and manufactured small gift items you might find in a souvenir or gift shop and was owned by two Italian brothers, Frank and Jerry Colapinto.

The Colapintos were people you would likely classify as "successful." They were involved in multiple businesses including several real estate ventures. Design Gifts was just one of their endeavors. Each night as I personally wiped down the desk of these successful brothers I would think to myself, "I want to be like that." Although I was only fifteen, I knew they had something that I needed. A certain quality, habit or characteristic that seem to set them apart; something that caused them to believe that success was possible for them. I wanted to know what that special something was, and I wanted to know if I could have it too.

After a few months of working with Brown's Janitorial, my boss asked me if I would be willing to work on a Saturday morning. Needing the extra money, I said yes. I met my boss at his home, and together we got into his truck and began to drive to a different location. I had no idea where we were going until we pulled up to this large home, and I asked him, "What are we doing here?" He responded, "This is Frank Colapinto's house; he hired us to help him move some items out of his garage today." Up to that point I hadn't been thrilled about working on a Saturday, but knowing I was about to meet Frank Colapinto made it all worth it.

We got out of the truck, and Mr. Colapinto greeted us at the front of the garage. He shook the hand of my boss and then looked to me. He stuck out his hand, and I quickly responded by putting my hand out to greet him as well. As we proceeded with the handshake he looked at me and said, "Frank Colapinto." I had never had anyone greet me by saying their first and last name, and I also had never heard anyone say their name with such confidence, self assurance and pride. It was just a "Handshake," but it changed my life forever.

Frank showed us a few things that he wanted done, and then he left to run some errands. The man I had admired from a distance said only two words to me but I will never forget them. Not necessarily what he said, but how he said it. A few hours later, after we were done with the work, I remember riding in the truck and thinking to myself, "could this be it...could this be the reason for his success?" Could it be that the only thing that separated Frank Colapinto from many others was confidence? Can something that small make that big of a difference? It was the only conclusion I could come up with. So I decided right then, that from that point on, when I was introducing myself to someone, I would say with confidence, "Chris Sonksen."

> Greatness is not an inheritance

For some strange reason that handshake made me believe that greatness was possible for anyone who wanted it. That it wasn't reserved for the elite or the upper class, but what separated the great from everyone else wasn't necessarily talent or skill... it was choice. For Frank Colapinto it was the choice of confidence that he displayed and a belief in himself.

It's funny my wife and I have been married for 19 years and just recently she said, "Why do you always say your first and last name when you introduce yourself?" I explained to her the story of how I first met Frank Colapinto, and how that meeting changed my life.

A few months later, I was having a conversation with my friends Conrad and Jill Padilla, and they mentioned the name Frank Colapinto. With such a unique name I figured it had to be him that they were referring to. After digging a little more, I found out that it was in fact the same man. They had become friends with the man whose handshake had changed my life nearly three decades before. I asked them to set up an appointment so I could meet with him, and they did.

A few weeks later I pulled up to a small restaurant to meet Frank (along with our friends Conrad and Jill) for breakfast. I walked in and there he sat comfortably in a booth reading the morning newspaper. My wife joined us just a few minutes later and when he greeted her he stood up, stuck his hand out and said, "Frank Colapinto." It probably didn't mean much to anyone else at the table, but in my heart it meant everything. It brought me back to a single moment that made a fifteen year old boy feel that success was possible for him.

> It is not the blowing of the wind that determines your success but it is the setting of the sail.

That's what this book is all about. It was written to help you realize that success isn't always about talent or skill. That greatness is not an inheritance. It's about the fact that the things the "great" do that others don't, are things you can do for yourself, in your own life. It's usually the little things that create the gap between those who are good or average and those who are really great.

The late author and speaker Jim Rohn once said, "It is not the blowing of the wind that determines your success but it is the setting of the sail." Everyone will face the wind, but where you end up is determined by how you set your sail. It's the little adjustments that makes the big difference. Adjustments might be things such as: attitude, commitment, focus, personal development, courage, character or mindset. My hope is that as you read through this book you make the adjustments necessary to bring your life to a level of greatness that you never thought possible. That the next person you meet will forever remember your handshake!

Contemplate, Evaluate, Activate:

Who has been an example of consistent confidence in your life?

_____

_____

_____

_____

_____

Are you a confident person in all areas of your life? Do others view you as a confident person? If not, what areas are you insecure or hesitant?

_____

_____

_____

_____

_____

What areas of your life do you already know need adjustments in order to achieve greatness?

_____

_____

_____

_____

_____

2

THE CHOICE OF A WINNING ATTITUDE
Bill Porter

Bill Porter wakes up each up morning and gets ready for work like millions of other Americans. He is in the sales industry just like thousands of other men and women across the United States. However, there is one slight difference; each morning it takes Bill three hours to get ready and to arrive to his territory. He stops by the shoe stand and every morning the shoe shiner ties his shoes. He then stops by the local hotel and the doorman buttons his top button and clips on his tie. This happens every work day because Bill Porter has cerebral palsy, which impacts his nervous system and affects his ability to talk, walk and fully control his limbs.

It started the day he was born in 1932, when the doctors used forceps and accidentally crushed a portion of Bill's brain. The damage from his birth left Bill with the cerebral palsy that he has battled his entire life. Growing up, most people thought Bill was mentally deficient. The government labeled him as "unemployable," and experts told him he would never be able to work.

Throughout his life his mother encouraged him and often told him "Bill you can do it, if you work hard enough you can become independent." These words shaped his life and developed a determination in him to become a contributing part of the work force. This imbedded in him a winning attitude that helped him see past his problem and to believe that more was possible for his life.

Bill's winning attitude gave him the confidence to apply for a job as a salesperson for the Fuller Brush Company. The company turned him down, saying that his disability would get in the way of carrying a sample case. This news did not discourage Bill from his desire to work. He next tried the Watkins Company! They agreed to bring him on as a salesperson but with one condition, he had to take the Portland Oregon territory. It was an opportunity, so Bill took it.

In 1959, Bill Porter rang his first doorbell as a salesman for the Watkins Company. The homeowner wasn't interested. He went to the second home and had the same result, they weren't interested. Bill's winning attitude wouldn't allow him to stop. He continued believing the best and hoping for the best and the sales began to come in!

Each day Bill covered 10 miles hauling around his heavy sample case, with his useless right arm tucked behind him. Whenever he would close a sale, his customers would have to fill out the order form because Bill has difficulty holding a pen. He pounded the cement day after day, exhausted, joints aching and his head suffering from migraines. He lays his head down on the pillow, sets his alarm for 4:45 a.m. and then does it all over again.

> Decide what you want out of life; look on the positive side; and never give up until you achieve it.

After nearly forty years of faithful service, being the only door to door salesman that Watkins still had, the company honored him with the prestigious Special Chairman's Award of Dedication and Commitment in the summer of 1996. During the presentation Bill's co-workers rose to their feet with a thunderous standing ovation. The cheers and tears from those in the audience lasted nearly five minutes.

Bill has become an icon in the world of business. Books are being written about him, a T.V. movie was made about his life and he is receiving the accolades that are long overdue. Bill put his remedy for success in these words "Decide what you want out of life; look on the positive side; and never give up until you achieve it."

Bill shows us that although life may not deal us the hand we would prefer if you find the positive side and be determined to keep your attitude right, you can win!

I am a firm believer that a winning attitude can truly set you apart. I believe the words of King Solomon when he said, "Your thoughts shape your life." It's true! There is nothing that will shape your life more profoundly than the attitude you choose to have! Attitude can separate winners from losers, victory from defeat, smiles from frowns and joy from sadness. It is a driving force in your life that, when properly adjusted, can give you the leading edge! I love the words of author/speaker John Maxwell when he wrote the following about attitude:

What is an attitude?

It is the "advance man" of our true selves.

Its roots are inward but its fruit is outward.

It is our best friend or our worst enemy.

It is more honest and more consistent than our words.

It is an outward look based on past experiences.

It is a thing which draws people to us or repels them.

It is never content until it is expressed.

It is the librarian of our past.

It is the speaker of our present.

It is the prophet of our future.

In short, attitude is a powerful dictator, and it literally has the ability to control every area of our life. Our marriages, relationships, careers, financial status, happiness, faith, success, achievements, education and overall fullness of life can be directed by the choices we make with our attitude.

FACTS ABOUT ATTITUDE

FACT #1 – Attitude is a choice

You may not be able to control what happens to you. However, like Bill Porter, you can control your attitude toward the circumstance. It's true! As a matter fact you can put two people in the same exact situation and you will get two different results. The results will vary based on their attitude toward it.

I remember traveling with a close friend of mine in his brand new Mercedes. This is the kind of car that you are afraid to breathe in. We had traveled for quite some time when we decided to pull off to the side of the road for some refreshments. We went into the store to get some snacks, and after paying the cashier we got back into his car. He put his new car in reverse, looked over his shoulder and began to back up. Within a few seconds I heard a loud noise. I took a quick look outside the passenger window and he had backed up into a small pole with his brand new Mercedes. Without any words being spoken, he put it in drive and took off. I said to him, "Aren't you going to get out and look at the damage." He said, "No, looking at the damage will only upset me and what is done is done…looking at it won't fix it.

> You cannot always choose your circumstances but you can always choose your attitude!

I probably would have made the mistake of getting out of the car and looking at the damage, allowing the circumstance to ruin my attitude. Two people in the car, same circumstance, different reaction.

Attitude is a choice. You cannot always choose your circumstances but you can always choose your attitude! Viktor Frankl said, "Everything can be taken from a man but one thing: the last of human freedoms – to choose one's attitude in any given set of circumstances – to choose one's own way."

FACT #2 – Attitude directly affects your success

In July of 1984, the Summer Olympics came to Los Angeles. It was an exciting time as the world's best gathered to compete. The media was camped throughout the city, writing stories, taking pictures and doing countless interviews. One article that ran during the Olympics was posted in the Los Angles Times. The article was all about the history of the Olympics, those that have won and lost and the moments of triumph that only the memories of the Olympic Games could possess. At the end of the article the reporter wrote these words, *"Throughout history the difference between the*

Gold and the Silver has come down to an average of less then 1/10th of one second. That's not talent, that's attitude."

Attitude can do that. It can be the difference between Gold and Silver or first and second. It can be the difference in a business transaction, a promotion or a raise. Attitude can literally bring you success!

Let's say for a moment that your boss has given you an assignment. You are to conduct the interviews and hire the person for the new position being offered by your company. You receive several resumes, do countless interviews and you finally narrow down the choice to just two candidates. As you begin to interview these two individuals you come to realize how similar they are. Their skills, education and general experience is about the same. They're the same age, same gender and have the same amount of passion. However, there is one thing that separates them, one has a highly positive attitude and one has an average attitude at best.

> Whether the attitude is good or bad makes no difference, it is contagious and those that come in contact with it will be affected!

Which one will you select as the new employee for your company? Chances are you will choose the one with the winning attitude. You know that they will get along better with their co-workers, they will treat customers better, they are less likely to complain or be critical and they are more likely to be loyal. In short, the person with the winning attitude wins!

FACT #3 – Attitudes are contagious

Years ago Dustin Hoffman starred in a movie called "Outbreak." The movie centered on an epidemic that swept across the nation, killing people within hours of contracting the virus. The most alarming part of the movie came when they discovered that the virus had gone "air born." In short, the virus had become highly contagious and affected anyone around!

It is the same with attitude; it is highly contagious and affects everyone around. Whether the attitude is good or bad makes no difference, it is contagious and those that come in contact with it will be affected!

There are two sets of rules that you must realize when it comes to a contagious attitude:

a) People will catch your attitude

Most likely you have heard the phrase, "your attitude is like a thermostat, it sets the temperature in the room." Whether it is the room of your marriage, relationship with your kids or the work environment, your attitude is contagious. If it is positive, it will bring out the positive in others, if it is negative, it will bring out the negative in others. Your attitude has the ability to build up or to tear down. You don't have to even say anything at times; your attitude will speak loudly what you feel.

> There are two keys that determine who we are: who we conceive ourselves to be and who we associate with."

b) You will catch other people's attitude

I recently read a great quote that was signed anonymous. It said, "There are two keys that determine who we are: who we conceive ourselves to be and who we associate with." If those closest to you are negative individuals who are always complaining, never grateful and have very few kind words to say, then chances are you will become like them. On the flip side, if you associate yourself with positive people, who believe the best, choose their words wisely and have an outstanding perspective on life, then chances are you will become like them.

Association is a powerful friend or detrimental foe. Allow only those who have a superior attitude to have influence in your life. In your work, business, church and circle of friends choose positive people with only the best attitude to be part of your life, because whether you like it or not, you will become like those closest to you

Fact #4 – Attitude is a learned response

Your attitude is not something that you were born with; it is a learned response. Similar to the natural act of walking, talking, eating and drinking, your attitude has become a mindless reaction...you respond without even thinking.

Your attitude was most likely shaped by one or more of the following:

a) Parents

You watched your parent's attitude toward life and the situations that happened to them. Maybe you watched how they talked about the boss or the people on the job. Maybe you viewed how they responded to each other or to the grind of daily life. Maybe they expressed that life never treated them fairly. Once again, whether it was good or bad, your attitude has been partly learned from your parents.

b) Teacher or Coaches

As you grew up there were other adults such as a teacher or coach that had a hand in shaping your attitude. It could have been the way they treated you, spoke to you, or the way they made you feel. But somewhere along the line a teacher or coach assisted in making your attitude a learned response.

> You can actually change any part of your attitude no matter how long it has been part of your life

c) Boss or co-worker

Your place of employment may have shaped the attitude you now possess. The boss who either has lifted you up or has pushed you down. The co-worker who has been either an encouraging or discouraging voice in your life. These voices have taken place most likely in your adult life, and they have reinforced your attitude toward life.

d) Friends

The friends you have had over the years have played a big role in shaping your attitude. As you think back, you can remember those who added to your life, but you can also remember those who took away from your life. Intentionally or unintentionally friends shape our lives and our attitude toward it.

The good news is that if your attitude is a learned response then that means it can be unlearned. You can actually change any part of your attitude no matter how long it has been part of your life.

Complete the exercise below:

Write your name with your writing hand. Then write your name with the opposite hand.

Writing Hand   Other Hand

Your probably noticed three things about writing with your opposite hand:

a) It was hard to do

b) It took longer

c) It looks lousy

With your opposite hand it was difficult, but with your writing hand it was easy. Your writing has become a learned response over the years; your opposite hand has not learned the same response. If you took time to write with your opposite hand it would most likely improve and become more of a natural response.

That is what needs to happen with your attitude. Work on the areas you struggle with until it becomes a natural response. Here are some ideas about reversing our attitude from the life of Bill Porter.

LESSONS ON ATTITUDE FROM BILL PORTER

1) Evaluate your attitude

If you saw the movie "Door to Door", (the story of Bill Porter) you would see how Bill continually had to evaluate his attitude. Every day he faced challenges and obstacles that would deteriorate the attitude of most people. His cerebral palsy, the continuing pain brought on by the hard toll of a door to door salesman and the numerous daily functions that you and I take for granted. Each day Bill Porter chose to keep his attitude in check. He did not allow the pressure of his life to overwhelm his attitude.

I encourage you to do the same. First, take an honest evaluation of your attitude. Are you negative or positive? Do you see the best or the worst? Be honest about your attitude toward life, people, your job, relationships, circumstances and your response when things don't go your way.

> You cannot have a life in the plus if you have an attitude in the minus.

Often, when we think of the word "attitude" we think of someone else. Someone in our office or at home, an acquaintance or a close friend, but rarely do we ever think of ourselves. However, if you would look deep inside your life and be honest with yourself, you will most likely find areas where your attitude struggles.

Below is a list of statements that will help to reveal if there needs to be an attitude adjustment in you. Put a checkmark next to the ones that describe you. Take this quiz slowly and really think it through; your honesty and transparency may help you shine light on an area of your life that desperately needs it.

___ I am critical.

___ I am focused on the negative.

___ I am short tempered with people.

___ I am quickly irritated by others.

___ I am quick to find faults.

___ I am a complainer.

___ I am a person who speaks poorly of others.

If you marked one or more areas above that may be a sign that you need to look deeper into your life and discover if there are any attitude issues.

You cannot have a life in the plus if you have an attitude in the minus. Attitude is something to place great value on. Evaluating his attitude was a daily practice for Bill Porter; it helped make him great.

2) Stop involving myself with negative circles

Due to the brain damage inflicted at birth, the government declared Bill Porter "unemployable." I wonder how many other people declared him unable to function in life. There had to be school yard bullies and neighborhood kids that teased him and made him feel like an outcast. I'm sure teachers in his life caused him to feel like he could never hold down a job or live on his own. Most everyone believed he would be forced to be a recipient of the government's system.

Bill Porter had to make a choice. Was he going to allow these negative influences to be a compass for his life, or was he going to stay away from them? Fortunately for Bill Porter he did not let the people in his life have the final word for his destiny.

Years ago, a group of scientists placed ten monkeys in a room with a batch of bananas at the top of a pole. The trick however, was that if a monkey climbed the pole and touched a banana he would receive an electric shock. The first monkey climbed the pole and received a shock and immediately climbed back down. The scientist then took that monkey out of the room and replaced it with another monkey, who knew nothing about the shock. When the new monkey wanted to climb the other monkeys would hold him down. The scientist began replacing one monkey at a time. Soon the original ten monkeys were gone and there were ten new ones. The ten new ones saw the bananas but knew nothing about the electric shock.

The experiment revealed that each time the scientist brought in a new monkey, the others would prevent him from climbing. The interesting part is that the new monkeys that held him down had no idea why they were doing it. They simply followed the pattern of those that were already in the room.

What a great lesson about nature. People will hold you down, but have no idea why. They will prevent you from climbing, because somewhere along the line they were prevented from climbing. If they aren't going to the top, they're going to stop anyone else who is trying to get there.

The hard fact is that there are people in your circle that are negative, and these negative influences can ultimately hold you down. Be careful with these people. You may need to limit your time with these individuals so that you can work on a healthier attitude. Choose your circle of influence wisely.

3) Choose to have a "Best Day" mentality

Our hero on the subject of attitude (Bill Porter) exemplifies the "Best Day" mentality. Everyday it took him three hours to get ready for work. So he made a mental choice that each day would be the best day. When he would stop and receive assistance to tie his shoes or put on his tie, he made the choice that, that day would be the best day.

You can read every book on attitude, attend every seminar and listen to every audio presentation on the subject, but there is no greater way of saying it, "attitude is a mental choice." Your mindset will direct your attitude.

Jesus Christ was recorded in Matthew 7:7 as saying, "Seek and you shall find." What a great truth. Whatever you seek you will find. If you go to work everyday believing that you will be passed up on promotion, thinking that you are treated unfairly, feeling like this is the worst place to be, that is the reality you will find. But, if you go to work believing that you will be productive, that good things will happen and that you will advance and grow, you will find those things. Because whatever you seek you will find.

If you wake up every morning and think, "Today is going to be a lousy day, I'm tired, I don't want to go to work and I don't feel good." You will find it. But if you wake up and say "Today is going to be a great day, opportunity will come knocking and I know something good is going to happen." You will find that as well. Because whatever you seek, you will find.

Fight hard at having a great mental attitude. It may not come naturally to you at first, but if you work at it eventually it will. If you truly want to raise the standard of your life, then you must raise the standard of your attitude.

Contemplate, Evaluate, Activate:

1. Is your attitude something people would want to "catch"?

_____

_____

_____

_____

_____

2. When presented with a less than ideal situation, do you first think of what is wrong, or do you look at what is right and look for solutions?

_____

_____

_____

_____

_____

3. Think about your friends, family, acquaintances, co-workers etc. Thinking about attitudes, is there anyone with whom you should spend less time, or completely discontinue contact?

_____

_____

_____

_____

_____

Action Steps:

Complete the exercises listed in this chapter. Again if you are not sure how to evaluate yourself, ask someone you trust to assist you.

3

THE CHOICE OF FOCUS
Jesse Owens

The sounds of a vibrant crowd hushed as he took the field. Hundreds of cameras fired off shots. The few cameras that could capture live action footage focused on his every move. The 1936 Olympics in Germany set the stage for one of the greatest moments in sports history and athletic irony. Black Olympic runner Jesse Owens loaded into the starting blocks.

As the gun sounded in this controversy-filled Olympics, one of the worst segregationists the world had ever seen, watched with great interest. This sociological scourge, Adolph Hitler, seethed, as a non-white athlete, Jesse Owens, earned four gold medals.

The race for the gold in Jesse's life superseded any Olympic venue. The race in his life was for racial equality through athletic excellence. Having studied the elements and tools Jesse used to get there, it is quite obvious he had many gifts, talents, and abilities. However, looking at each of those, a subtle thread, a distinct trait held together the tapestry of greatness.

Jesse Owens had a sharpened focus on reaching the goals that he set in his life.

The seventh of 10 children James Cleveland Owens was born to Henry and Emma Owens of Danville, Alabama on September 12, 1913. The family lived in a small unheated home. Often there was not enough food to feed them all. Education was put on hold so the brothers could work with their father in the cotton fields attempting to bring in enough money to make ends meet. After years of struggling and in hope of a better life, Henry Owens sold his tools and the farming animals and moved to Cleveland, Ohio.

On the first day of school, young Owens was asked by the teacher, "What's your name?" Timid in his response, "J.C." was whispered. The teacher wrote down "Jesse" and the name stuck for the rest of his life.

It was in grade school that Jesse discovered his unique athletic ability… Jesse could run.

Over the next few years, Jesse continued to work odd jobs to help his family, while attending grade school and racing against his friends. At age twelve, Jesse entered Fairview Junior High School. Charles Riley, the track coach for the school, was astonished when at age twelve Jesse ran the 100-yard dash in 10 seconds flat. It was obvious to the coach, teachers and students that this was no ordinary child. Yet deep in the heartland, the racial heat of segregation often clouded and concealed his natural athletic ability.

> Jesse Owens had a sharpened focus on reaching the goals that he set in his life.

During high school Jesse continued to work hard to help support his family, and in those days of hardship Jesse learned to embrace his ability to compete and to remain focused before the starting gun.

Jesse won every major track event including winning the state championship three years in a row. During Jesse's senior year, at the National Interscholastic Meet, he set the world record for high schools, running the 220-yard dash in only 20.7 seconds. Jesse realized that becoming a professional athlete would have its share of challenges, but would be his only way to ever get ahead. He learned that he had to remain focused on the goal or the tension and trials around him would crush him.

While enrolled at Ohio State University in 1933, he paid his tuition by working three jobs in addition to his studies and track activities. As the foundations of global stardom were applied to Jesse and his athletic ability, the sad reality of local segregation weighed heavy in every aspect of his life.

Along with all the other black athletes, Jesse was required to ride to the meets in separate vehicles from the white athletes. They were forced to live off campus and when they traveled, they stayed in "Black Only" hotels and had to eat in "Black Only" restaurants. The prejudicial tension that Jesse felt, the demanding schedule of school, training, and three jobs sharpened his focus. His single-mindedness was strengthened. He sharpened his focus giving him a satellite shot of his future dreams. He was determined not to allow the surrounding circumstances to dim his vision for the future.

On a cool day in May, in the spring of 1935, Owens traveled to Ann Arbor, Michigan, for the annual Big Ten Track and Field Championships. Only a few months prior, Jesse had hurt his back. Recovering, but still in pain, his coach talked to him about missing the meet. However, Jesse was determined that he would participate. New York Times columnist, Arthur Daley called Owens's performance at Ann Arbor "the greatest day in track history." In less than an hour of competition, the young athlete tied the world record for the 100-yard dash, broke the world record with a long jump of more than 26 feet, broke the world record in the 220-yard dash and broke another world record in the 220-yard low hurdles.

In pain, and submerged in desperate adversity, Jesse excelled.

Three world records shattered. One tied. The world was introduced to "Jesse" with the megaphone of monumental focus. It seemed that making a way to win when there was a world of odds against him became his signature. Perhaps it was a complex metaphor of his own life; winning against all odds because of a determination birthed from focus.

News of Jesse's unbelievable performance spread through the country and with the Olympics only a year away, Americans began to pin their hopes on the star from Ohio State. Jesse continued to train, overcoming obstacles, and defeating odds that would cause most people to quit.

He believed in himself.

He believed in his dream.

He never lost focus.

The stage was set for the 1936 Olympics. While Hitler hovered in his perch, the brand new Nazi facility was Germany's pride. Athletes from all over the world gathered to compete and discover who the best in their sport was.

For Jesse this was the paycheck from all the part time jobs. This was the platform for potential equality from racial tension. Prejudice would have to recognize greatness. It was time to introduce the spectacular Jesse Owens to the world.

During the Olympics, Owens excelled beyond the expectations Americans had pinned on him. His footprint was pressed into the mold of Olympic greatness by winning a total of four gold medals.

> He believed in himself. He believed in his dream. He never lost focus.

He took gold in the 100-meter sprint.

He took gold in the 200-meter sprint.

He took gold in the long jump and the 400-meter relay.

Journalist Pete Axthelm, later wrote about Jesse's Olympic performance.

"He didn't merely run and jump to four gold medal victories in the Berlin Games of 1936. He took flight, soaring far above a world of athletic competition, enlarging the possibilities of the sport itself."

Jesse Owens is an American icon and one of the most famous and symbolic heroes in Olympic history. He not only had an unprecedented athletic gift, but he also possessed an inner quality called focus. Jesse knew what he wanted and year after year he worked toward this dream. Despite whatever occurred around him, he remained focused.

I travel a lot. I meet many people. In my encounters I have seen greatness missed because of one's inability to remain steadfast on a goal, assignment, mission or task. Add to this a lethargic approach to purpose and potential, many great moments are missed because of a lack of attention.

If faced with Jesse's challenges, many people would have used the excuse of busyness as the reason they did not succeed. I have heard sabotage spoken from people whose life is like a bee in a tin can. They ricochet moment by moment, never really capturing the focus needed for a significant snapshot. Some use the excuse of a bad upbringing. I have heard people say that they came from a poor family, and that they couldn't work to support the family and work toward their dream at the same time.

Racial prejudice is a tragedy in America. When I look at Jesse's life, I am encouraged by his example of how he overcame such a force. Some have faced much less than racial inequality and still floundered.

I have heard people say, "I would never have made it through college because I didn't have support from my family; they wouldn't let me succeed." That same person will most likely never experience success in business or career either. Why? A lack of focus. Those without focus use excuses as the weapon against effectiveness. Either way many people would have found a way to excuse themselves from their dream and allow their conscience to accept less than what was possible.

Jesse Owens was different. Jesse chose to be focused and it served him well in his career as an athlete.

People cannot become great in the future if they are not willing to practice focus in the present. Owens didn't wake up one day in his mid-twenties and say "I'm going to be a Gold Medalist." He decided early on in life that he would use his God-given talent and mix it with self discipline. This was his edge.

Focus is the practice that is needed for a man like Edison, who tried over and over again, to make his experiment work. It was focus that drove Mary Kay Ash to build a cosmetic empire that empowers thousands of women around the world. It was focus that made a young boy named Steven Spielberg borrow his dad's camera to produce his own home movies with the dream that someday his ideas would come to life on the big screen. Focus is what's needed to keep the passion burning for a young girl who trains every morning at 4:00 a.m. in a cold ice skating rink. Choosing focus, is something the great do that others don't. It's in their mind - focus. In their heart - focus. In their soul and spirit - focus. It drives them to keep moving forward regardless of what lies ahead.

In my chosen profession I have the opportunity to meet several types of people. I have noticed that when it comes to focus, everyone falls into one of the five following categories. See if you can identify which one you fall into...

No Focus

There are many people who have absolutely no focus in their life. They don't have any direction and they leave destiny to chance. To them focus is a button on a camera that when pushed brings great results. Yet in reality, it is more than a button. It's a belief. Those with no focus over look this. Whether they are troubled from the past, deal with massive insecurities, are unmotivated, or simply lazy, they lack clear focus. They may possess gifts and abilities, sometimes beyond those who are focused, but because they lack focus for their own life, they find themselves making little or no progress.

These people often have tremendous potential, but they are like a Christmas gift that is never opened. It remains wrapped in paper and neatly placed in a box, far from the reach of greatness. The gift remains unseen and its potential remains untapped.

Partial Focus

The second group has focus but does not change. These people differ from the previous, but the result is still the same. They have a faded idea of how they see their life developing but they do not take the necessary steps to make anything significant happen! Their focus is limited to the here and now. They are limited because they cannot see past today. They are unwilling to work for tomorrow. The person who has little focus in their life but doesn't make any changes, will be left with a small vision that has no roots.

> People cannot become great in the future if they are not willing to practice focus in the present.

Unfinished Focus

Years ago I met a young man at a seminar I was teaching. He told me of his dreams and his desire to achieve a level of greatness in his life. In a few short minutes, I gave him some quick advice that I believe, if acted upon, would have helped him begin the journey toward his dream. I walked away from that conversation and quite honestly gave it very little thought. About a year later I was teaching at another seminar when I was approached by someone who looked very familiar to me. As I began to speak with this person and listen to their story, I realized it was the same young man from the year before. As I reflected on our conversation, it occurred to me that this fellow had done nothing with the advice I had given him. Possibly moved with good intentions, he never activated the plans because he lacked focus.

He had focus in his life, but his focus had no follow through.

Many fall into this category. They have a dream, an idea, a vision for their life but they have no follow through. Imagine someone saying, "Someday I'll win the gold medal in the Olympics," but not train everyday to get there. Focus is an absolute necessity for success. If you don't accompany the focus with follow through then your dreams and goals will be categorized under the file of "things I never did."

Seasonal Focus

Another popular problem among people is that their focus is lived out in seasons. In other words, their ability to focus is like a light switch that can be turned on and off. Sometimes it's on and sometimes it's off. This type of person is strong for a season and during that time it seems as if nothing can stop them. Then, without any warning, they stop focusing and lose sight. They begin to drift. Once they are drifting, something must occur to trigger the switch back on. Something must motivate them to refocus.

This is a better place to be in, because at least in certain seasons of your life you are making progress. However, if you want to be among the great, the cycle must stop. You cannot be partially focused and expect complete results. Seasonally focused people must take practical steps to break the trend and become consistent in their ability to stay centered on the task.

Clear Focus

This person knows exactly where they are headed and is willing to pay the daily price to get there. They are not easily swayed from their vision! They face the same circumstances as most people, but they do not allow those circumstances to get them off track. If anything, they use the circumstances as fuel to keep them moving forward.

Clearly focused people do not necessarily possess greater gifts than those who have little or no focus.

Mention the name Michael Jordan, most likely you know who I am talking about. However, if I mention the name Leroy Smith, you probably have no idea of whom I am referring to. In 1978, at Laney High School in Wilmington, North Carolina, Leroy Smith beat out Michael Jordan for the only sophomore spot on the Varsity Basketball team. Coach Fred Lynch spoke about Jordan:

> *"He didn't sulk or threaten to quit when he had to settle for the Junior Varsity team. He just started working out harder and improving his game. If anything, it made him more determined."*

This describes a person with clear focus. This is the heart of a person that will find a way to succeed.

As a sophomore in high school Michael Jordan could have easily said "I'm done playing basketball, I can't handle the let downs." But he didn't, he worked harder and improved his ability. He stayed focused on his dream.

Jesse Owens. Michael Jordan. People you know. People I know.

Focus is vitally important to the overall achievement of our personal lives. Now, let's look at some specific, practical lessons from the life of Jesse Owens.

FIVE LESSONS ON FOCUS FROM JESSE OWENS

Know and Choose What You Want

Jesse Owens knew exactly what he wanted… to be a professional athlete. He determined early on in life that he would be one of the greatest. He was determined to break the poverty stricken life that bound his youth. His talent was a natural God-given gift but defining what he wanted was a choice.

Choice is a crucial part of each individual's personal success; to have a clear understanding of what it is they are attempting to achieve. The goal is not as important as the clarity that you have for that goal. It may be an achievement that is possibly one, three, five or ten years away. In this first step, the size of the goal and the tasks it takes to complete it is not important.

What is important is that you know what you want to achieve.

Determine What It Will Take To Get There

Once focused on the goal, it is important to define the steps that it will take to get you there. When Jesse Owens decided that he wanted to be a professional athlete that was a great goal. But a goal doesn't mean anything if there is no action put to the goal. He worked so he could attend Ohio State. That was an action step. When he trained in the early morning hours and did his studies late into the night that was action.

> His talent was a natural God-given gift but defining what he wanted was a choice.

You can have all the focus you want on the finish line, but if you don't start running you will never get there!

Robyn Allen, former president and CEO of the Insurance Corporation of British Columbia said:

> *"Many of us are afraid to follow our passion, to pursue what we want most because it means taking risks and even facing failure. But to pursue your passion with all your heart and soul is success in itself. The greatest failure is to have never really tried."*

Once you know what you want to do, create a plan to get it done, and have the focus and passion to follow through.

Think "Can" not "Cannot"

People are experts at talking themselves out of their own dreams. They list reasons why they should not pursue their personal dreams or goals.

Jesse Owens was someone who had every reason to say "I can't" but still decided to say "I can." Racial tension, financial struggles, and many other obstacles stood between him and his desires. However, he refused to accept those problems as reasons to stop!

I love the story of Vietnam veteran Bob Wieland. Bob had natural athletic ability and possessed a dream of having a life long career in sports. Athletic competition was the joy and passion of Bob's heart. He went to war and those dreams shattered when he lost both legs in battle. Unlike most people, Bob refused to become bitter or angry. His legs were gone but not his focus and an "I can" spirit.

He was determined to have a place in sports. Over the next few years Bob began to train and exercise, building up the muscle in his arms. He learned to walk on his hands and he accomplished a three year walk across America.

He raced across America on a custom made bicycle.

He completed the New York and Los Angeles marathons.

He competed in and finished the Hawaiian Ironman Triathlon.

He also bench pressed an astounding 507 pounds.

Bob is a remarkable example of a man who had every reason to say "I can't." But he refused to accept defeat; he worked hard, kept his focus and achieved his dreams.

Find a Focus Coach

Find someone to keep you focused. This may be someone who is already your mentor, or it may be someone entirely different. A Focus Coach is someone that helps you to remain focused in order to accomplish the goals you have in your life. For Jesse Owens that person was Charles Riley. Remember, that it was Coach Riley who was the track coach at Fairview Junior High School. He helped Jesse keep his focus, when everything around him could have easily pulled him away.

> A goal doesn't mean anything if there is no action put to the goal.

Every person, regardless of who they are, can get off track, can lose focus, and take their eye off the goal. It is essential and necessary for anyone who wants to achieve any level of greatness to find someone who can keep them accountable and focused on the task.

Here is a helpful habit I learned from my focus coach. Each year I write out my personal goals. These goals include the things I want to achieve throughout the year. I give a copy to my personal mentors, and I ask them to keep me accountable throughout the year. I want them to help me stay focused and faithful to the course!

Anyone who wants to be great and successful will take this step seriously. Find someone to hold you accountable to being focused.

When Knocked Down, Get Up

This final piece of advice from our hero Jesse Owens may sound like a cliché. If and when you get knocked down, get back up. However, it is advice that is easier said than done. Most people will get knocked down and stay down. They get bitter, resentful, depressed, defeated, insecure, unmotivated, and often feel like a failure. Ultimately, they allow what knocked them down to keep them down!

Create the type of courage that will withstand a hard hit, but keep moving forward with single-mindedness and unwavering focus. Combine focus and follow through to help you to arrive at your destiny; success.

Let me conclude this chapter with the words of Thomas Paine:

"The harder the conflict, the more glorious the triumph. What we obtain too cheap, we esteem too lightly; it is dearness only that gives everything its value. I love the man that can smile in trouble, that can gather strength from distress and grow brave by reflection. 'Tis the business of little minds to shrink; but he whose heart is firm, and whose conscience approves his conduct, will pursue his principles unto death."Action Step:

If you do not already have one, find someone to be your Focus Coach. This may or may not be someone who is currently a mentor in your life. Arrange a meeting with your coach to discuss steps to improve your focus. Create action steps and a system of accountability.

Contemplate, Evaluate, Activate:

1. What excuses have you used or are you currently using for not pursuing your dreams and goals?

_____

_____

_____

_____

_____

2. Which of the four focus categories (No Focus, Partial, Unfinished, Seasonal, or Clear) would you place yourself?

_____

_____

_____

_____

_____

Action Step:

If you do not already have one, find someone to be your Focus Coach. This may or may not be someone who is currently a mentor in your life. Arrange a meeting with your coach to discuss steps to improve your focus. Create action steps and a system of accountability.

4

THE CHOICE OF PERSONAL DEVELOPMENT
Sally Kristen Ride

Have you ever looked up at the night sky and wondered with a child like awe, what would it be like to fly around in space? What would it feel like to be closer to the stars and the moon, to see one entire side of the earth? To feel the forces of a man made machine launch you from the safety of the ground into an unknown world. The thrill of launching, the adventure of journeying to uncharted territory, to feel fear and excitement as they join together in your emotions creating a sense of anticipation that you have never felt before

For most of us this is only a dream. A journey that most individuals will never take! For Sally Kristen Ride, this journey became a reality. On June 18, 1983, Dr. Ride became the first woman ever to be launched into space. Her six day, two hour flight was a great success! It was an experience that Dr. Ride will never forget. However, the journey into space started long before 1983.

The journey started at the young age of eighteen when in 1969, Sally enrolled herself into the Swarthmore College in Pennsylvania to study science. She had a desire to learn, to expand her mind and to develop her potential. She worked hard everyday as she began her pursuit of a degree.

Later she changed schools and began attending Stanford University in California. After many years Sally graduated from Stanford with degrees both in English and Physics, an accomplishment that only an individual committed to personal development could achieve. With a superior education from one of the finest Universities in the nation, Sally made a choice to continue her pursuit in the world of Physics. She enrolled into graduate school and it was there that she received her PhD in astrophysics.

While attending graduate school, her endless pursuit of personal development was proven again when she applied to be an astronaut at the National Aeronautics and Space Administration (NASA). At that time 8,900 people applied with great hopes to be accepted for training through the NASA program. Of the 8,900 individuals who applied only 208 were accepted. Sally Kristen Ride was one of those people! The application process continued with a rigorous training program and then in January of 1978, NASA announced that Dr. Ride was one of only 35 people who had been selected for the astronaut program!

After completing training in January 1979, Dr. Ride served in two important NASA positions after her training. The first position was as a crew member in a chase plane for shuttle flights. The other was as a Capcom (capsule communicator) from the ground to the shuttle. Then in April of 1982, her years of personal development had a giant pay off when NASA announced that she was selected to be part of the crew for the STS-7, or seventh shuttle flight, on the Challenger space shuttle.

> When you realize that learning and growing is a life long journey you will see that along the way opportunity will knock and you will be prepared for it.

This announcement made history! Sally Kristen Ride would become the first woman to ever journey into space. Her years of hard work, late night studying, and pursuit of personal growth had paid off in a way that maybe she had never imagined. Dr. Ride's choice to pursue personal development placed her in the history books and opened the door to a journey that most will never experience.

Her six day, two hour flight into space in June of 1983 was a giant success! All that NASA had hoped to accomplish was completed. Although the journey into space had ended in just six short days, the journey of personal growth and development for Sally had just begun.

She left the astronaut corps in 1987. From there she joined the faculty of Stanford University and then in 1989 she began working as a professor at the University of California in San Diego, where she also heads up the California Space Institute. Dr. Ride was committed to further her learning experience by passing on her wisdom to students studying in the field of science. Since 1989, Dr. Ride has written several books including a children's book entitled To Space and Back describing her experiences in space. An additional book entitled Voyager: An Adventure to the Edge of the Solar System and a third book she calls The Third Planet: Exploring the Earth from Space.

Personal development will open doors for you just as it did for Sally Kristen Ride. It will open the doors of opportunity and allow you to walk through them. When you realize that learning and growing is a life long journey you will see that along the way opportunity will knock and you will be prepared for it.

Imagine a soldier not being prepared for battle. They haven't prepared physically or mentally, they have not trained in the area of combat, they have not learned the skill of being a great soldier. Will they be ready when duty calls? NO! Will their chance of survival and success be decreased because of their lack of preparation? YES! As they run to the battle will this thought go through their mind "I wish I had prepared."

Your battle may not be on the field of war but it may be in the school you attend, the company you work for or the business you hope to start. Either way…you better be prepared! Personal development is not an event, it is a lifetime journey.

IF PERSONAL DEVELOPMENT IS SO GREAT THEN WHY AREN'T MORE PEOPLE DOING IT?

Through my travel and speaking commitments, I have come to realize that most people do not choose ongoing Personal Development for one or more of the following reasons:

1) Underestimate the need for growth

They don't see the need or recognize the importance for personal development. For them learning ended the day they walked out of high school or college. They don't see the benefits and they underestimate the power of personal development.

2) Overestimate their knowledge

They have a higher opinion of themselves than most! They have learned a great deal in their field and they believe that they are superior to their peers. They have put learning on the back burner and rely on old knowledge to get them through.

3) Love the idea, but hate the work

There are those individuals who really do see the value of personal development! However, their good intentions aren't good enough. The idea of personal development is a great one, but they are unwilling to translate it into a winning habit in their life.

> When personal growth becomes part of your daily life, other avenues of success are sure to follow.

4) Relying too much on past successes

Pastor and author Rick Warren says "The greatest enemy of tomorrow's success is today's success." He is absolutely right! Many people feel that they have obtained a level of success in their life and don't feel the need to learn anymore. This backwards thinking creates a barrier for future successes.

THE BENEFITS OF PERSONAL DEVELOPMENT

I remember years ago when I decided that personal development would become a constant in my life. Through a variety of resources I began to develop personally, and I immediately saw a change in my life. I was thinking clearer, having greater ideas, feeling more alive. It created a spark in me that I had never felt before.

The following are some great benefits you can look forward to if you choose to pursue personal development:

PREPARES YOU FOR FUTURE OPPORTUNITIES

Opportunity may knock on everyone's door but only a few can answer. The few are those who have taken the time to develop their life on a daily basis. Our hero in this chapter is a perfect example. Dr. Ride had the opportunity to become a candidate for the NASA program and ultimately become the first woman in space. Her commitment to personal growth opened the door for opportunity.

KEEPS YOU AHEAD OF THE GAME

The great Spanish composer-cellist Pablo Casals was in the final years of his life and a reporter asked him this question, "Mr. Casals, you are ninety five years old and the greatest cellist that ever lived. Why do you still practice six hours a day?" Pablo Casals answered him "Because I think I'm making progress."

That is the heart of someone who has made personal development a lifelong journey. They see the benefit of continually learning and they realize that it will help them stay ahead of the game!

CREATES OTHER AVENUES

When personal growth becomes part of your daily life, other avenues of success are sure to follow. Your mind will expand, your influence will increase and advancement in your career will become more likely. There's a greater chance of financial gain, new tasks being given to you and your skills will undoubtedly be sharpened.

These are just a few of the avenues of success that personal development will open up to you. So the reality is that you have a choice! You can choose to stay the same or you can choose to grow. But if you do the same thing the same way, don't expect different results! I am a firm believer that successful and unsuccessful people do not

> The greatest enemy of tomorrow's success is today's success.

vary much in their abilities. They vary in their desire to reach their fullest potential.

If you have a desire to be great in your own life then develop a plan for personal growth. Make it something you do daily. Something that simply becomes part of your fiber! That's what created success for Sally Kristen Ride and that's what will do it for you. She was committed to personal growth and the results have been a life full of great successes.

LESSONS FROM SALLY KRISTEN RIDE ON THE PRACTICE OF PERSONAL DEVELOPMENT

1) Choose to grow

Right now decide in your heart and mind that you are going to choose to grow! That personal development and growth will become part of your daily life. That you are not going to allow busyness, fatigue, or any other unworthy excuse to get in your way.

In the movie "Bridges of Madison County" the character, Franchesca, played by Meryl Streep made a statement that fits in this chapter so perfectly. She said, "We are the choices we make." What a simple and yet profound realization. You and I become the choices we make. Choices about love, faith, values, relationships, family and priorities all make up who we become. But in addition to these valuable life decisions, are also the choices you and I have to make about personal growth.

2) Create a plan for growth

Dr. Ride not only chose growth, she also created a plan. Choosing to grow is only the first step...you must also create a plan.

In my opinion, this is where most people fail. They start off with great zeal, committing to everyone around them that they are going on a journey of growth. They take all the necessary steps, pack all the right items, announce their departure, but then never leave the station. The reason they do this is because they have not put a realistic plan of growth into place. Earl Nightingale once said, "If a person will spend one hour a day on the same subject for five years, that person will be an expert on that subject." Imagine if you spent an hour a day on personal growth, your life would absolutely positively improve. Here are some things you can do right now to put your choice of growth to work:

a) Read books, blogs and other print media – Read all you can on personal growth and development. Read about the subjects you need to grow in.

b) Listen to audios, podcasts, etc. – There are audio books, seminars and other forms of teaching you can listen to that can greatly increase your personal development.

c) Associate with people farther along than you – Find people who are farther down the journey of personal growth and spend time with them. By simply being around them, they will keep you encouraged and moving forward.

d) Attend conferences/seminars – There are great conferences and seminars that by attending would boost your personal development.

e) Seek out a personal development mentor – This person would meet with you regularly and hold you accountable to your personal growth journey.

You might be saying this sounds great, but my life is already extremely busy. Here are some ways that you could find time for personal growth:

> If a person will spend one hour a day on the same subject for five years, that person will be an expert on that subject.

a) Wake up a little earlier and devote that time to personal growth. If you woke up an hour earlier everyday or even 30 minutes, could you imagine how much you could learn in just one year? Try it out and watch it work…you will grow faster than you think.

b) Take advantage of the dead time you have and spend it growing. There is so much time wasted throughout our weeks. Stop and think how much time you spend waiting in line, waiting at airports, waiting in a doctor's office, waiting for an appointment, on lunch breaks or traveling on a plane. Keep a book with you because you never know when you can read a chapter or two while you wait.

c) Time spent in your car – In Southern California, where I live, the average person spends 1 ½ hours on the freeway every day. Chances are you spend some time in a car everyday. Now imagine if you had teaching books on audio and you listen to those rather than the radio. You could gain as much as 6-8 hours per week in personal growth by simply switching what you listen to in the car.

3) Be consistent

Whatever path you choose for personal growth you must be consistent. It is easy to allow a week to become a month and a month to become a year. Soon you realize that you're back where you started. Napoleon Hill said "It's not what you are going to do, but it's what you are doing now that counts." You might choose to grow and then implement a plan, but if you are not consistent then you will not see the results.

Personal development is a lot like physical development. If you desire to be physically fit, you must make a choice and you must devise a plan, but if you are inconsistent you will not reap the benefits. The same is true with your personal growth, if you want to see results you have to stay consistent.

4) Don't let accomplishment slow you down

A horrible trap in the journey of personal growth is letting your current or past successes slow you down. What happens is that we begin to experience a certain level of achievement and we become complacent at that level.

Sally Kristen Ride could have felt that many times. When she achieved two degrees at the same time she didn't allow her success to become her enemy. She moved on to graduate school and earned her PhD. She continued to grow by becoming an astronaut for the NASA space program. Even after becoming the first woman in space, she started a whole new learning journey by becoming a well noted author. She could have stopped at any one of her success stages and rested in her accomplishment, but she didn't, she kept moving forward on the journey of personal growth. Don't let your success be your enemy, keep growing and more success will come your way!

5) Remain teachable

Often when I do a public speaking engagement I watch the body language of people in the audience. Some sit on the edge of their seat ready to learn and grow. They are taking notes, asking questions, wanting to expand their minds and sharpen their skills. They possess in them a desire for growth. It's a passion and you can see it in their eyes!

Then there are those in the audience with their arms crossed. Everything about their body language and expressions tell me that they feel they have nothing more to learn. They may be at the seminar out of habit or have been forced to attend, but they have ended their personal growth journey and are now simply going through the motions.

As you continue down your personal growth journey make sure you remain teachable. Don't ever come to the place where you feel you have arrived. Learn from every situation, book, CD, conference, seminar, speaker, accountability partner, mentor, personal trainer and any other avenue of growth that comes your way. Whether you are 20 or 80 or any age in between, never be through with learning. Because when you are through with learning, you are truly through.

Contemplate, Evaluate, Activate:

1. In what ways are you actively seeking personal development? Be specific.

_____

_____

_____

_____

_____

2. If you are not currently seeking personal growth, beyond reading this book, what steps can you take to bring personal growth into your daily life?

_____

_____

_____

_____

_____

3. Are you teachable? Really think about this. If you are not sure, ask someone you trust.

_____

_____

_____

_____

_____

5

THE CHOICE OF ADDING VALUE TO OTHERS
Howard Schultz

A while back an organization I founded was holding a leadership conference in the state of New Mexico. It was early in the morning and the incredible staff I am privileged to work with was making last minute preparations. With still two hours to go before the conference began I thought it would be a great leadership move to go and buy coffee for everyone on the team. I grabbed the M.C. of our conferences, my good friend Jason Harper, we got directions from a local resident to the nearest Starbucks and we became two men on a mission.

After 40 minutes, two more sets of directions, and passing several other coffee shops along the way we found ourselves outside a closed mall that housed the only Starbucks in town. Because of our schedule we could not wait for the mall to open. We peeked through the windows and actually saw the Starbucks. We were so close and yet so far.

As we headed back to the conference location, Jason and I began to laugh at ourselves. How determined we had become to get the coffee from the local Starbucks, and how no other coffee would do. We began to discuss what made Starbucks different, why America is so wrapped up in this company. The organization seemed to be set apart from everyone else. They are in a league all their own. But what are the choices that have helped them achieve such greatness?

It all started in 1981 when Howard Schultz was serving as vice president at Hammarplast – a Swedish maker of stylish kitchen equipment and housewares. Schultz took notice of a small company in Washington State that was ordering a large number of a special type of coffee maker. Schultz's curiosity in this company got the best of him and he boarded a plane and headed to Seattle. He fell in love with the company and their overwhelming care in choosing and roasting the perfect beans. He was impressed with the owner's dedication to educating the public about the wonders of coffee connoisseurship.

A year later Shultz convinced the owners to hire him, and he became the director of marketing and operations for the Starbucks Company. Schultz, however, had another epiphany. This one occurred in Italy, when Schultz took note of the coffee bars that existed on practically every block. He noticed that they not only served excellent espresso, they also served as meeting places or public squares. With over 200,000 of them in the country, they were a big part of Italy's societal glue.

But back in Seattle, the Starbucks owners resisted Schultz's plans to serve coffee in the stores saying they didn't want to get into the restaurant business. With his vision in his heart, Schultz left the Starbucks Company to open a string of specialty coffee stores in Seattle modeled after the typical Italian espresso bar. Schultz quickly raised $400,000 in seed capital and by the end of 1986 he had $1.25 million in equity (including backing from his former Starbucks partners). While Schultz's stores

> When you determine to be "others" minded, you have made a decision that will alter your life.

took off, only a year later in 1987, Schultz bought the original Starbucks franchise. Between 1987 and 1992, Starbucks, under Schultz, opened 150 new stores. By September of 2009 Schultz was operating stores in more than 50 countries, through more than 16,000 stores around the world.

Schultz always said that the main goal was, "to serve a great cup of coffee." But attached to this goal was a principle: Schultz said he wanted "to build a company with soul." This led to a series of practices that were unprecedented in retail. Schultz insisted that all employees working at least 20 hours a week get comprehensive health coverage. Then he introduced an employee stock-option plan. These moves boosted loyalty and led to extremely low worker turnover.

In addition to his practice of adding value to his workers Schultz has worked hard to add value to humanity. Under his leadership Starbucks adopted an environmental mission statement and pledges to buy only coffee that has been organically grown. The company has built schools, health clinics, and has worked with celebrities such as Magic Johnson to open stores in urban neighborhoods. The Starbucks Foundation sponsors literacy programs, Earth Day clean ups and regional AIDS walks.

The drive to continually add value stems from his childhood and watching his father work in an unhealthy, non-appreciative environment. Schultz said of his father, "He was beaten down, he wasn't respected. He had no health insurance and he had no workers compensation when he got hurt on the job." So with Starbucks Schultz said he would, "build the kind of company that my father never got a chance to work for, in which people were respected."

Starbucks has achieved what many thought impossible under the umbrella that if you add value to people, value will be added to you. In a society that is self-driven, adding value to people may seem like a waste of time. Those who think that way have no clue to the power that comes from this practice. When you determine to be "others" minded, you have made a decision that will alter your life.

Let me give you just a few benefits that come from adding value to those around you:

a) You deposit success into others

When you add value to people, and work hard at bringing out the best, you are depositing in their success. You are playing a dream maker in their life and helping them on their journey to the top.

b) You build your network

Networking is a powerful tool in any organization and adding value is the quickest way to grow your network. If you choose to add value to people, your circle of friends and those you can count on will grow.

c) You build loyalty

Nothing will increase the loyalty of those you serve and of those who serve you then adding value. When you add value to people they become loyal to you. This happens because they feel better about themselves when they are around you. Because of this value they feel they will be loyal to you and will protect you when others try to hurt you.

d) You build longevity

Schultz made it a mission to add value and the result has been a very low turnover rate in his company. Most people who work on the retail side of Starbucks are not well paid, but because of the value they feel they stay with the company. Adding value creates longevity.

> When you fail to recognize the benefit that comes from adding value to others, you have begun the process of subtracting whether you realize it or not.

e) You create a winning atmosphere

It is a fact…people operate better under the banner of value. They are more productive, less likely to complain and more likely to be problem solvers instead of problem makers. If you want to have a winning atmosphere, start adding value to those around you.

f) You increase your level of influence

We all know that leadership is influence, and there is no greater way to gain influence in people's lives than when you show value to them. When an individual feels appreciated and valued by someone else, that person gains a larger influence in their life.

g) You will receive a great return on your investment

When you sow value into people's lives you reap value in your own. When you begin to regularly, unselfishly add value to others, you gain so much in return. You gain people who will be loyal to you, fight for you and defend you. When people feel that you have invested in them, they will in return invest in you. That is the law of sowing and reaping.

The benefits from adding value to others is tremendous. But just as you win when you add, you lose when you subtract. When you fail to recognize the benefit that comes from adding value to others, you have begun the process of subtracting whether you realize it or not.

Howard Schultz has modeled for us that adding value to others is a characteristic that has made him great, and it will do the same for you. Here are some ideas that you can begin to implement that will assist you in adding value to your most precious resource...people.

LESSONS FROM HOWARD SCHULTZ ON ADDING VALUE TO OTHERS

1) Discover simple ways to provide a daily touch

I was recently reading an article about a CEO of a mid-size company that desired to add value to his people by providing a daily touch. He realized that spending a large amount of time with each employee was not possible. However, he realized that each person needed a small touch to show them their value. This CEO decided that every Monday morning he would visit each desk, cubicle and office and drop off a piece of candy. You might be thinking, "big deal a piece of candy." But as this creative leader dropped off a piece of candy he would share a few words with each person. This is a deliberate and conscious effort to provide a daily touch each week.

It's a lot easier to ask for a 'hand' if you have taken the time to touch a 'heart.' If you want to add value to people you have to find ways to touch their heart and encourage their spirits. The larger your organization is the more difficult this becomes, but if you get creative you can figure out a way.

On an episode of 'Primetime, American Made' Howard Schultz and the Starbucks company was featured. During the episode they visited a local Starbucks and interviewed the manager. The gentleman was asked about his opinion of Howard Schultz. His reply was genuinely positive. He shared with the reporter how he had an opportunity to meet Mr. Schultz and how he has received communication with him on occasion. It was obvious to anyone watching the program that the local store manager had value added to him by the CEO of Starbucks and it was accomplished as a result of touching the heart.

Get creative! Find ways to touch the heart of people. Who knows...it maybe as simple as a piece of candy.

2) Find the need and fill it

Remember at the beginning of this chapter how we learned that Howard Schultz has made it a mission of Starbucks to provide medical benefits and stock options for his employees. He doesn't have to do this, but Howard Schultz realizes that if you want to gain the benefits that adding value to others will give you, you must be willing to find the needs of your people and fill them.

> The best way to get ahead is to teach the person below how to get ahead

Too often, leaders forget that the team is their roadmap to success, keep them happy and you will win. They overlook pay raises, benefits, vacations and other practical items that are needed for the person to feel valued and appreciated.

Gary Feldmar, president and sole owner of Excello Press, a 25 million dollar printing company in Chicago, built his company on good human relations. Here are some examples of how he adds value to his people by finding the needs in their life and filling it:

- When the son of his sales manager was hurt trying to break up a fight in school, Gary sent the youngster a book on body building and self-defense.

- When he hired a new manager, the man's wife received a bouquet of flowers to welcome her to the company.

- When one of his salesmen was putting in long hours traveling to take care of customers, Gary learned that his salesman was having marital problems. He promptly gave the salesman and his wife a two week vacation and he picked up the tab. Mr. Feldmar said of the incident, "So it cost the company…it was what he needed and we want to keep our people happy."

This is how a true leader works. They find the needs of those on their team and do what they can to fill it. The needs you fill may vary. It may be a pay raise that's over due, a bonus that needs to be rewarded or simply flowers to the spouse at home to let them know you care. Begin doing this and you are on your way to reaping the benefits that adding value rewards.

3) Platform others for success

To platform others is to give away the credit, to allow someone else to win or to give responsibility away. It is to train someone to do the job that you do, to raise them up and to allow them to shine outside of your shadow.

Most people find this very difficult and the primary reason is fear. Fear of letting someone else shine brighter than you. Fear that someone else may do the job better than you. Fear that if you give away the responsibility there will be nothing left for you to do. These are signs of insecure leaders who are failing to see that true leadership platforms others for success, that by pushing others up, you yourself will be lifted up.

David K. David expressed this idea when he said, "The best way to get ahead is to teach the person below how to get ahead. You never get promoted when no one else knows how to do what you do now. Most people get promoted because they get pushed up from underneath rather than pulled up to the top."

Years ago I worked with an organization called "On Fire." This organization traveled throughout the United States speaking to America's teens through the public school system. My job on the team was to play the role of the host. I would take the first ten minutes of a public school assembly and interact with the teenagers through music and games. Then I would hand the microphone over to Donny Burleson.

After about a year of playing host, we were sitting in a restaurant having dinner and he said to me, "Why don't you speak tomorrow morning?" I thought to myself, "Are you out of your mind? You're the speaker to teens not me." He spent the next few minutes encouraging me and helping me to write out some thoughts. The next day came and before I knew what hit me I was standing up in front of 500 teenagers. Now I love to speak, but speaking at a public school assembly is much different then a leadership conference. Donny is one of the best in the nation for speaking to teens, but on that day he stepped aside

> It is a wise practice for a leader to bring something to the table for his team.

and helped to platform me for greater success.

When you platform others you add value to them and you increase your impact and influence in their life. The greatest job security you can ever have is when you have mastered the art of lifting people up. Discover ways to lift people outside of your shadow and you will be well on your way to adding value to those around you.

4) Bring something to the table

I grew up in a fairly large family; there were five of us kids plus Mom and Dad. My dad worked in construction and my mom was a homemaker. It was a great thing as a child to walk home from school and know my mom would be there. Mom always cooked dinner for the entire family. She would set out a table with seven places and prepare a meal to feed us all. She was and is a great cook and I always looked forward to the meals she would lovingly prepare for us. I could always count on her bringing to the table something that was good, fresh, and prepared with love.

Similar to a mother who brings something to the table, it is a wise practice for a leader to bring something to the table for his team. It is not something that feeds their physical body, but their soul and spirit as a leader. It is something that educates the team and brings out the best in them. What I mean by this is the leader brings articles, books, newspaper clippings, magazines, brochures on conferences or any other item that would add value to their team. When you resource people you are adding value to them and you are becoming part of the process for their success journey.

Remember that Howard Schultz didn't decide to start adding value when his company reached greatness, he started adding value in the beginning and that is what has taken him to the top. That is what will take you to the top.

Contemplate, Evaluate, Activate:

1. Are you making a conscious effort to add value to the people in your life?

_____

_____

2. What are some practical things you can do to add value daily to...
Your spouse:

_____

_____

    Your children:

_____

_____

    Employees/coworkers:

_____

_____

    Business partners:

_____

_____

3. Actively look for "needs" and fill them. Document your "need filling" for one week.

Day 1 _____

Day 2 _____

Day 3 _____

Day 4 _____

Day 5 _____

Day 6 _____

Day 7 _____

6

THE CHOICE OF CHARACTER
Coach John Wooden

There is nothing quite like the thrill of sports. The players, fans, announcers and last minute comebacks make sports exciting events to watch. To sit on the edge of your seat as your team scores the last second winning goal, run or shot. Whatever your sport, games are a thrill to watch. America is rich with sporting history and electrifying moments. One individual who brought America hundreds of "holding your breath and biting your nails" memories was the late, great Coach John Wooden. His contribution to sports in this country is legendary. The work he did and the person he was will be long remembered.

He is one of only two players to go into the Basketball Hall of Fame as both player and coach, as a player in 1961 and then as a coach in 1973. He has broken countless records, has been named "Coach of the Year", "Sportsman of the Year" and has left a winning streak that has not yet been touched. He is a man of character, quality and excellence. He is an achiever and he believes that each man has a responsibility to reach his fullest potential. He once said "Don't measure yourself by what you have accomplished, but by what you should have accomplished with your ability." Coach John Wooden is a legend in the World of Sports and he has made his mark in history.

His love for the sport began at age 8 when John took a pair of his mother's pantyhose, stuffed them with rags and made a makeshift ball. This was his humble introduction to a sport that would change his life. He continued practicing at the old farm until he made it on the Martinsville High

School basketball team, where he enjoyed an All State career. He then made his way to Purdue University where he would inherit the nickname "Indiana Rubber Man" given to him for his suicidal dives on the court.

Under the guidance of Purdue's head coach Ward "Piggy" Lambert, Wooden led the team to the national championship. It was at Purdue where John Wooden became a three time Helms Athletic Foundation All American and was named Player of the Year in 1932. After his time at Purdue was finished, Wooden focused his attention on his passion of coaching and began the career that would become the benchmark for all other coaches to follow.

> Be more concerned with your character than your reputation, because your character is what you really are; your reputation is merely what others think you are.

He spent two years coaching at Dayton High School and nine years at South Bend Central High School, compiling an impressive 218-42 record. Wooden then went on to coach at Indiana State University, where he recorded a two year 44-15 mark. Wooden's big break came in 1948, when he accepted the head coaching position at UCLA. For 15 years Wooden laid the groundwork for what would become the dynasty of dynasties. Here is a list of accomplishments achieved by what many consider the greatest coach ever:

- UCLA record under Coach Wooden 620-147
- Led Bruins to four 30-0 seasons (1963-64, 1966-67, 1971-72, 1972-73)
- Led Bruins to 88 consecutive victories
- Led Bruins to 38 straight NCAA tournament victories
- Led Bruins to 149-2 record at Pauley Pavilion
- Led Bruins to 19 PAC 10 championships
- Led Bruins to 10 national championships including seven in a row (1966-73)
- NCAA College Basketball Coach of the Year six times (1964, 1967,

1969, 1970, 1972, 1973)

- The Sporting News Sportsman of the Year (1970)
- Sports Illustrated Sportsman of the Year (1973)
- During forty years of coaching compiled a 885-203 (.813) record

Coach John Wooden set a standard for a winning tradition. He has left a legacy of coaching, teaching and motivating others to become everything they possibly could be. He is a leader and he knows how to rally people to success.

However, there is one characteristic that has set him apart; one fundamental belief that has served as a pillar in his personal and professional life. Simply put... Coach John Wooden is a person of character. He was quoted as saying, "Be more concerned with your character than your reputation, because your character is what you really are; your reputation is merely what others think you are."

Think about it for a moment. There are so many attributes that you could consider when speaking of Coach John Wooden. You could talk about his winning tradition, the need for possessing a positive attitude, or team building. You could easily talk about the importance of adding value to others, and lifting the lid of potential to those of whom you associate. The list could go on and on regarding the qualities found in Coach John Wooden and the lessons we could learn about success. However, the one that stands out above the rest is character. You see it's his character that has become the foundation by which all the other successes have been built.

Character is what is inside of you; it's who you are when no one is looking. It is the foundation on which your entire life is truly built. It is more than what people perceive, it is the real you.

You could have a fancy car, big house, large savings account and an entire list of accolades, but it is surface success at best without the depth of character behind it. Character matters! Famous author and speaker Zig Ziglar once wrote about a survey taken among vice presidents of large corporations throughout America. After a series of questions and interviews, the studies revealed that the executives who practiced character where more likely to be happier, healthier and more successful. You see if you want to experience true success -character matters.

James Kouzes and Barry Posner interviewed CEO's and managers in thousands of case studies and recorded their findings in the book, The Leadership Challenge. The number one characteristic of admired leaders according to these case studies was honesty. They wrote, "It's clear that if we're to willingly follow someone – whether it be into battle or into the boardroom, into the classroom or into the back room, into the front office or to the front lines – we first want to assure ourselves that the person is worthy of trust. We want to know that the person is being truthful, ethical and principled." Character is what has set apart truly successful people like Coach John Wooden and that is what will set you apart as well.

> You will have great peace knowing that your life is an open book and you have nothing to hide.

Just think about the benefits you receive when you choose character as a foundation for your life.

1) Clear conscience

What a great benefit to living a life of character, a clear conscience. Never having to lie to cover up where you have been, what you have been doing or who you were with. You will have great peace knowing that your life is an open book and you have nothing to hide.

I have a 16 year old son and he is one of those kids who doesn't like to hide anything. He cannot deal with holding back a secret that he knows he should share. This is a great quality and I hope he continues to possess it throughout his life. A few years ago, he came to my wife and shared with her that he was with his friends riding his bike on our cul-de-sac and he and his friend went down the street and crossed over another street. This is something he knew we would not approve of. It took him a few days to tell us, but when he did he shared it with great remorse.

I asked my son about the situation and shared with him that we love him and would never want anything bad to happen. He understood but then he shared something I will never forget. He said, "Dad, the worst thing about crossing the street was not telling you in the last few days. I thought about it all the time and it was hard for me to fall asleep at night because I knew I needed to share it with you. I feel so much better now that I have told you."

This is exactly what I am talking about. The benefit of character is a clear conscience. You don't have to worry about being discovered or losing any sleep because you know you have been honest.

2) Builds trust

Have you ever bought anything from a salesperson only to find out that the item you had purchased did not work like he or she had promised? When that happens, what do you think about that person? They were not honest with you, they have no character and because of that I will not easily trust them again.

The opposite would be true as well. Trust can be established when character can be counted on. If you have character you will have trust with people, if you don't you won't. It's that simple!

Trust can be built when you have the following characteristics:

- Make a commitment and keep it
- Be on time for meetings
- Follow through with the phone call
- Finish tasks on time
- Use time wisely
- Manage personal and business finances well

> If you have character you will have trust with people, if you don't you won't. It's that simple

This kind of character builds trust, and when you build trust the rewards are great.

3) Higher quality of relationships

Relationships are driven by character, whether in the corporate world or in the privacy of your own home, the quality of your relationships improves when you are a person of character.

Character is important when you are parenting as well. Your character will affect your children's view of you, which will ultimately affect their lives. In Volume 12, Number 1 of the Executive Speechwriter Newsletter the article reads:

"When I told my kids to clean their rooms, they took a closer look at the condition of my tools and possessions in the garage. When I told them that honesty was our family's greatest virtue, they commented on the radar detector I had installed in my car. When I told them about the vices of drinking and wild parties, they watched from the upstairs balcony at the way our guests behaved at our adult functions. Integrity is easier preached than practiced and children are especially good at seeing the differences between what their parents preach and what their parents practice."

4) Greater success

Character breeds success. Think about it for a moment. Who do you want to buy a car from? Whom do you want to sell your house, do your taxes, and invest your money, someone with character or someone you can't trust? And who will get the most repeat business, someone with character or someone you can't trust?

If you have broken trust with a client not only are you likely to lose their business but also the business of those they know. Word of mouth is powerful. If they don't like you and can't trust you they will also tell their friends. If you want to build great success, be a person of character.

Strong character will also bring greater joy and health into your life. Without the inner strife of wrestling between who you are and who others think you are there will be a limit on the amount of joy you will experience. Greater health will result from eliminating the stress of a dual life. Your stress will be limited, your mind will be at ease and your spirit will be enveloped with a calm peace. All of these benefits come from becoming a person of character.

Author and speaker Dr. Jay Strack expressed:

"Time changes things, sometimes drastically. Styles change, as do expectations, salaries, communications systems, styles of relating to people. But some things have no business changing, like respect for authority, personal integrity,

wholesome thoughts, pure words, clean living, love for family and authentic ser-
vanthood. Character qualities are never up for grabs. Times must change, but
character never."

Character is a timeless principle for anyone desiring greatness. Our way of doing business may change over the years, but the value of character can never change. It will forever be an element for success.

Below are some practical steps you can take to become a person of character. If you will put into place these qualities, you will assure yourself of building a foundation of character and be on your way to greatness.

LESSONS WE CAN LEARN ON CHARACTER FROM COACH JOHN WOODEN

1) Make the right thing non-negotiable

This is the first and foremost step in becoming a person of character... be committed to the right thing and never negotiate with it. What I am talking about is morals and standards. Telling the truth, honest business dealings, faithful relationships, priority of family, obeying the laws, kindness to others, forgiving people, love without condition...these should be non-negotiable.

> Integrity is
> easier
> preached than
> practiced

It is tempting at times, to give in and not hold true to these values, especially when you can personally benefit. You may be faced with a situation that if you lie, it saves you from trouble, if you cheat a little, you will save a lot of money, and if you are dishonest, you will close the business deal. The benefit may come, but in the end you will ultimately pay. Decide right now not to sway from doing the right thing no matter how tempted you may become.

2) Treat people right

A person of character treats people right. Not only those you love but those you don't. This was a great quality of our hero in this chapter, Coach John Wooden. Countless former players speak of the honor to know him, because of the way he treated people. He brought out the best in them, believed in them and wanted them to succeed.

A couple of years ago, my family and I went with a few friends to do some dirt bike riding in the desert. In preparation for the trip I needed to do a few things to the R.V. that we owned at the time. I had to check the water, propane and battery. Everything was good to go except the battery that runs the inside lights was not working. I had just purchased the battery two months before so I knew it was under warranty, and so I took it back to the auto store where I purchased it.

With my receipt in one hand and the battery in the other, I headed into the store to take care of the battery situation. I told the lady behind the counter about my situation and she put the battery on the tester. The computer read, "Must charge battery and re-test." She proceeded to tell me, "We have to charge the battery and see if it will work before we can give you a new one. The only problem is we don't have a battery charger here, it is at our other store which is about 7 miles away." She continued by saying, "Maybe you can go and get the battery charger and bring it here or you can take the battery there."

Now, I have to be honest, I was a little upset, but I decided to keep my cool. She went into the backroom and a few minutes later she returned. She told me, "Sir, you have been more patient and kind than any other person I have helped today. I am going to give you a new battery, and you can be on your way." I was shocked. I had kept my mouth shut, and it paid off. You see I have a commitment to treat people right, but just like you I sometimes fail. I have learned that when I do treat people right it pays off. Let treating people right be part of your character, part of who you are, and I promise you will enjoy a great reward.

3) Keep your promises

Simply keeping your promises is about the easiest and most effective lesson you can ever have. If you have committed to do something, do it. Keeping your promises is about the most basic rule of character building you can follow, but when this principle is ignored the damage quickly multiplies.

It is a lot like building your credit. If you have ever purchased a home or an automobile, or if you have ever attempted to buy anything on credit, you know that the first thing the lending institution is going to do is "check your credit." Those with great credit can obtain almost anything they want; those with poor credit will find it much more difficult.

Have you ever stopped and wondered what a credit rating really is? It is simply a history report on your promises. Have you done what you said you would do? Those individuals who fulfilled their promises will find it easier to obtain a loan versus those who failed to keep their word. Character is about fulfilling your promises and the rewards are great.

I read a little story about a boss and an employee discussing integrity. The boss said, "Integrity and wisdom are essential to success in every business. By integrity, I mean when you promise a customer something, you must keep that promise even if you lose money." The employee responded, "And what is wisdom?" The boss quickly fired back, "Don't make any such fool promises."

What a true statement…be wise enough not to make a promise you can't keep. Keeping promises gives you character, opens up opportunity and builds trust. Do what you say you will do, be where you say you will be, arrive at the time you said you would be there. Follow this very simple rule and it will serve you well.

Contemplate, Evaluate, Activate:

1. Are you the same person no matter the person or people you are with? If not, explain.

_____

_____

_____

_____

_____

2. Is your conscience completely clear; is there something you should "confess" to someone?

_____

_____

_____

_____

3. What are some areas of your life (large or small) where people may not trust you?

_____

_____

_____

_____

Action Step: If there is anyone you have broken faith with, whether in a personal or business relationship, make amends. This may not always be possible, but do everything you can to make things right. Commit to be a person of integrity.

7

THE CHOICE OF THINKING BIG
Oprah Winfrey

One of the reasons people don't achieve their dreams is that they desire to change their results without changing their thinking. How you think will determine how you act and how you act will determine how others react to you. The way you think is powerful in regards to your future and the fruit your life produces. One person who understands the power of thinking big and understands that you must never let circumstances limit your thinking is the famous talk show host Oprah Winfrey.

Oprah was born January 29, 1954, to an unwed sixteen year old girl named Vernita Lee, who wasn't ready to be a mother. Oprah lived the first few years of her life on a farm with her grandparents in Kosciusko, Mississippi. From the time she was nine years old she was abused sexually by male family members and acquaintances. She did not speak of these tragic events until the 1980's when she revealed to America the horrifying truth of her childhood.

At age 14, Winfrey went to live with her father in Nashville, Tennessee, and it was there that her life was put back on track. Her father insisted on hard work and discipline as a means of self improvement, and Winfrey complied, winning a college scholarship that allowed her to attend Tennessee State University. While attending college she landed her first role in radio as the announcer for WVOL in Nashville.

Two years later after receiving her B.A. from Tennessee State, she became a reporter at WTVF-TV in Nashville. From 1976-1983 she lived in Baltimore, working for the ABC affiliate WJZ-TV, progressing from news anchor to co-host of the popular show, "People are Talking."

In 1984, she moved to Chicago and took over the ailing morning show, "A.M. Chicago." By September of the next year, the show was so successful that it was expanded to an hour format and renamed "The Oprah Winfrey Show". "The Oprah Winfrey Show" is one of the most popular television programs in history. Then, in 1986, Oprah continued expanding her impact by establishing Harpo, Inc., her own production company. ("Harpo" is "Oprah" spelled backwards) She has also established "O", a popular magazine produced by her company.

> Nothing limits achievements like small thinking; Nothing expands possibilities like unleashed thinking.

In 1991, motivated in part by memories of her own childhood abuse, she initiated a campaign to establish a national database of convicted child abusers and testified before a U.S. Senate Judiciary Committee on behalf of a National Child Protection Act. President Clinton signed the "Oprah Bill" into law in 1993, establishing the national database she had sought, which is now available to law enforcement agencies and concerned parties across the country.

On September 18, 1997, Oprah introduced her program known as "Oprah's Angel Network," which was designed to encourage her twenty million viewers to make the world a better place for all of us to live. Oprah told her viewers, "I want you to open your hearts, and see the world in a different way."

During its existence Oprah's Angel Network raised more than 80 million dollars, provided shoes and school uniforms, to more than 18,000 impoverished South African children, built 55 schools in 12 different countries, and since hurricanes Katrina and Rita, the Angel Network helped build or restore more than 400 homes in the gulf coast area.

Oprah's path that led from her grandmother's farm in Kosciusko, Mississippi to becoming the first African-American woman billionaire is a story of unwavering focus and the ability to think beyond her circumstances.

Oprah Winfrey serves as our hero in this chapter as someone who learned to think big. When education may have not happened without the hard work of earning a scholarship, she thought big. When others may have been limited by a painful past, she chose to think big. Seeing the needs of children and families, she established programs that would make a difference because she decided to think big.

William Arthur Ward claims, "Nothing limits achievements like small thinking; Nothing expands possibilities like unleashed thinking." We are limited by our thinking. In the case of Oprah Winfrey, she was faced with multiple issues that could have limited her thinking. She once said, "Nobody had any clue that my life could be anything but working in some factory or a cotton field in Mississippi." Others may have thought that about her, but she refused to accept that way of thinking.

> You have to think anyway, so why not think big.

That's what thinking big will do for you; it will shape your future into an image of success. It will bring you to a place that you were meant to be. Author David Schwartz expresses, "Where success is concerned, people are not measured in inches or pounds, or college degrees, or family background; they are measured by the size of their thinking."

When you stop and think about it, it is only you that limits yourself. It isn't your surroundings, background or upbringing. It isn't your age, gender or race. It isn't your abilities, talents or gifts. What limits you is your thinking. The intriguing part of this truth is that you cannot always control what happens to you, but you can control what happens through you.

There are hundreds of thoughts running through your inner dialogue every minute of every day. You are constantly thinking. That is the way the Great Creator made you. As long as you are alive and healthy you are thinking. Donald Trump says it this way, "You have to think anyway, so why not think big."

Oprah chose to think big when she was young, and she hasn't stopped. You have the ability to make the same choice. It is free to you! It won't cost you anything. You can begin to think bigger than you have ever thought for your life, career, success, marriage, family, dreams or goals.

THE REWARD OF THINKING BIG

Here are some rewards you can count on when you choose to think big:

1) Makes dreams possible

You were created to dream, and when you begin to think big, you begin the process of dreaming. A matter of fact, great dreams become nearly impossible for the person who doesn't think big. They say that dreams start in the heart, but really they start in the mind. When the person begins to think bigger than they ever have thought before, those thoughts formulate a dream that begins to possess the heart. With enough passion, drive and determination the dream that once seemed impossible, becomes possible.

Every great dream that has unfolded in history began with a person having an idea. A person that began to think bigger than other people thought. Computers, airplanes, restaurants, iPods, overnight mail, cell phones, copiers, automobiles and hundreds of other items in life that we enjoy are the direct result of someone thinking big.

Our limited thoughts are like a lid. They keep our dreams from flowing out and bubbling over. They limit our dreams and our realized potential. Don't be a lid to your potential. Don't let your thoughts keep you from becoming the person you were intended to be.

2) Opens opportunities

In the autobiography of Martin Luther King Jr., Dr. King tells of growing up in Atlanta, Georgia:

> *"I remember another experience I used to have in Atlanta. I went to high school on the other side of town – to the Booker T. Washington High School. I had to get the bus in what was known as the Fourth Ward and ride over the West Side. In those days, rigid patterns of segregation existed on the buses, so that Negroes had to sit in the back of buses. Whites were seated in the front, and often if whites didn't get on the buses, those seats were still reserved for whites only, so Negroes had to stand over empty seats. I would end up having to go to the back of that bus with my body, but every time I got on the bus I left my mind up on the front seat. And I said to myself, 'One of these days, I'm going to put my body up there where my mind is."*

And he did. Our bodies always end up where our minds are.

What a great lesson. If you want your life to end up somewhere great, then let your mind take you there. Big thinking does that, it opens up wonderful opportunities. People hire big thinkers, people rally around big thinkers, opportunities are presented to big thinkers. Big thinkers get big opportunities; small thinkers get small opportunities. It all starts in the decision you make to be a big thinker. Big thinking opens the door of opportunity for business, financial gain, ideas, books, songs, investments, dreams, goals and personal growth as well as organizational growth.

Konrad Adenauer said it this way, "We all live under the same sky, but we don't all have the same horizon." What separates people is often the way they choose to think.

3) Gathers the great

The church where I serve as the Lead Pastor has experienced some incredible growth. It was founded in 1998 and has been experiencing great progress year after year. In 2002, the church was only four years old, but we had a desire to build a main auditorium that could hold our growing congregation.

The time came for us to raise the initial funds to get the project moving. We had planned a special event that was to be held underneath a tent in the parking lot. The day before the event we experienced a terrible windstorm; the worse the city had seen in years. By 11:00 a.m. the entire tent had been destroyed. It was quite a sight to see. We rallied some people together, cleaned up the area and set up chairs out in the open.

> If you want your life to end up somewhere great, then let your mind take you there.

The next morning we held our event, and it was incredible. I was amazed at the type of people our event drew. The mayor was present, city councilmen, a variety of other city officials and several prominent business men and women also attended. We raised the funds necessary on that very special day and we moved forward with our project.

Over the 18 month process we continued to have businesses and business people step to the plate and contribute through financial donations as well as donating materials and labor. Why did they do this? What was their motive? Well it's simple; they wanted to be a part of something big. Big thinking always gathers great people. It has worked for me in every area of my life. Big thinking is simply a magnet for great people.

If you have a dream for your life or for your organization, then share it with people. Share it with passion and clarity. Let them see the incredible benefits that will happen when your dream turns into reality. If you can communicate it to people, show them a plan and what it will take to get there, your dreams will gather great people. You will find that people who are smarter than you, wiser than you, more talented than you and financially stronger than you will rally to your side and partner with you in seeing your dreams take flight. So think big, really big, and watch how some of the greatest people you have ever met join by your side and take your dreams all the way to the top.

4) Forces teamwork

This point flows perfectly from the previous point. Your big thinking will gather great people and you will need people to make it happen. You have heard it before, "big dreams require big teams."

My son, Aidan, loves to play baseball. His favorite thing to do is to pitch and being left handed really helps. I love to watch him play. I often tease people by saying that I am training my son to be a professional baseball player and that everyone has their form of retirement, well, my retirement is his left arm. On the baseball field, my son has learned the value of teamwork. He can be pitching a great game and putting the ball into plays that should be easy, however, if his team doesn't perform then it doesn't matter how well he is pitching. He is realizing that in order to achieve something great he needs other people's help.

Think about our featured guest in this chapter, Oprah Winfrey. She is talented, gifted, successful and wealthy. But when she decided to pioneer her work known as "Angel Network" she looked to her friends, colleagues and the nation for help. You see, if all she wanted to do was to continue being a host, she could have done that and done it well. But her thinking was much bigger, and when you think bigger it forces you to develop a team because you realize you cannot do it alone. There may be several things you can accomplish on your own, but fulfilling big dreams is not one of them. Charles de Gaulle said it best when he said, "Nothing great will ever be achieved without great men." If you're going to be a big thinker, be ready to be a team builder, because big thinking forces you to develop big teams.

5) Gives you influence

A few years ago, the world lost one of the greatest contributors to humanity, Mother Theresa. She was known worldwide for her compassion that was shown through feeding thousands, caring for the sick, providing shelter and housing lepers in India. She went there with a dream, not with resources and not with great finances, but with a dream in her heart, and the world took notice. Her influence was enormous. Politicians, celebrities and world leaders had great respect for this small in stature but large in thinking woman.

Mother Theresa's incredible influence was a direct result of her big thinking. She believed that she could provide care for thousands of forgotten people, and she did. You see that is what big thinking does. It gives you a place of influence, and influence is what gives you a place of leadership. Without influence you really are not a leader. I love the leadership proverb that says, "If you're leading but no one is following, then you're just taking a walk."

> If you're going to be a big thinker, be ready to be a team builder.

Understand that influence is not achieved by simply thinking big. In addition to thinking big, influence is achieved by other attributes such as character, integrity and a positive attitude. It is achieved by investing in people, encouraging people and bringing out the best in others. People are wired to dream big and when they find someone else dreaming big, they will often throw their time, talent and resources at any dream they find worthwhile... even if it isn't their own.

6) Turns circumstances into stepping stones

Big thinking has a way of blasting through obstacles that small thinking would find too difficult. This is true with someone you may or may not have ever heard about…Maxcy Filer. In 1966, he was thirty six years old when he took the bar exam for the very first time. Unfortunately, he didn't pass. So he decided to take it again and once more he didn't pass. He took the bar exam in Los Angeles, San Diego, Riverside, San Francisco and anywhere else it was given in California. Each time however, Maxcy failed.

After twenty five years, $50,000 in exam fees and 144 days spent in testing rooms, Maxcy Filer at age sixty one passed the bar on his forty eighth attempt. Most of us would be thinking about retirement at his age, but not him. Most people would have given up on the tenth, twentieth or thirtieth try, but not Maxcy. He said, "I couldn't possibly quit." That was his attitude then, and it continued to be his attitude as he began his practice in Compton, California. People know that when Maxcy Filer says he'll fight to the end for their case, they can take it to the bank. He doesn't give up!

That is what big thinking does for you. It gives you perseverance beyond anything you ever thought possible. It turns any circumstance you face into another stepping stone in your quest to reach your dreams. Big thinking propels you forward and keeps you moving forward. Big thinking creates the mindset that no matter how many times you fall, you always get back up.

7) Unleashes potential

I've heard it said, "If what you did yesterday still looks big to you, you haven't done much today." Big thinking forces you to do more than you have done before. When you begin to go after the dreams that have been produced by big thinking you find yourself doing things that you have never done before, excelling in areas that you have never even tried. Your potential has been pushed and you have risen to the occasion.

The motivational company Successories created an image of an iceberg. The image shows a small iceberg on top of the water, but the majority of the iceberg is pictured under the water. The motive behind the image is to inspire the viewer to see that there is more potential that lies inside of them that has yet to be seen.

The same is true of you. You have been made by your creator for great things, and as soon as you start the process of thinking big and going after those big thoughts, you will find a river of untapped potential that will pour out of you. You will begin to do things that you have never imagined and reach goals that you once thought impossible.

8) Promotes growth

Albert Einstein worked on several projects, failing many times but always learning and growing. Ben Franklin and Thomas Edison attempted hundreds of experiments, failing many times but always learning and growing. Dr. Seuss presented his work to many publishers who refused to help, failing many times but always learning and growing.

When you join the ranks of these big thinkers you are guaranteed one thing, you will learn more than you ever imagined. You will grow as a leader, innovator, creator, administrator, economist and many other avenues of growth you might have never reached without pursuing the dreams that big thinking produces.

> If what you did yesterday still looks big to you, you haven't done much today.

Over the years I have taken my share of risks. I have stepped out and tried what seemed impossible. Sometimes I failed and sometimes I succeeded, but I always learned. I always grew. I always became a stronger individual as a result of big thinking, and so will you.

Learn from legendary people like Oprah. See yourself as becoming more and doing more. There is greatness lying deep inside of you just waiting to get out and the only way to release it is to start thinking big. Always remember the leadership lesson from Henry Ford that I have gravitated to all my life, "whether you think you can or can't, you're right."

Contemplate, Evaluate, Activate:

1. Do you have big dreams? If so, list them. If not, Why not?

_____

_____

_____

_____

_____

2. Do you have a team in place to help you reach your dreams? List the key people on your team. If you have more than one team for different dreams, list each team separately.

_____

_____

_____

_____

_____

3. If you do not have teams in place who are some people you can approach to be a part of your team? Choose wisely.

_____

_____

_____

_____

_____

Contemplate, Evaluate, Activate:

4. What are some obstacles in your life that keep you from dreaming?

_____

_____

_____

_____

_____

8

THE CHOICE OF COURAGE
Amelia Earhart

I magine boarding an early model small plane with the intent of crossing a vast ocean. Now imagine that you intend do this alone, and you are traveling with the knowledge that only one other person has succeeded in this journey. This is the position that Amelia Earhart put herself in when she endeavored to be the first woman to fly solo across the Atlantic.

Amelia was born on July 2, 1897 in Atchison, Kansas. She had an early love for the world of aviation and possessed tremendous courage. Her flying career began in 1921 when at the age of 24 she took her first flying lesson from an instructor known as Neta Snook. The thrill of being in the air and floating through the sky was everything she had hoped it would be. Amelia loved to fly. She then purchased her first plane, a Kinner Airstar. However, due to family problems she was forced to sell her airplane in 1924 and moved back East, where she took employment as a social worker.

Four years later, she returned to aviation. She purchased an Avro Avian airplane and became the first woman to make a solo-return transcontinental flight. From that point forward, she continued to set and break her own speed and distance records, in competitive events, as well as personal stunts promoted by her husband, George Palmer Putnam.

Earhart's name became a household word in 1932 when she became the first woman and second person to fly solo across the Atlantic on the fifth anniversary of Charles Lindbergh's feat, flying a Lockheed Vega from Harbor Grace, Newfoundland to Londonderry, Ireland. That year she received the distinguished "Flying Cross" from the US Congress, the Cross Knight of the Legion of Honor from the French Government and the Gold Medal of the National Geographic Society from President Hoover.

In 1935, Earhart proved her incredible courage once again by becoming the first person to fly solo across the Pacific Ocean from Honolulu to Oakland, California. Later that year she soloed from Los Angeles to Mexico City and back to Newark, New Jersey. Her feats of courage continued to astonish the world as she was able to continue advancing in her personal achievements.

In July 1936, she took delivery of a Lockheed 10E "Electra," financed by Purdue University and started planning her round-the-world flight. Earhart's flight would not be the first to circle the globe, but it would be the longest – 29,000 miles, following an equatorial route. She boarded the plane for this record breaking flight with her navigator, Fred Noonan. They departed Miami on June 1, 1937 and after numerous stops in South America, Africa, the Subcontinent and Southeast

> Courage is the price that life exacts for granting peace with yourself.

Asia, they arrived at Lae, New Guinea on June 29. They had accomplished 22,000 miles in their journey. The remaining 7,000 miles would all be over the Pacific Ocean.

On July 2, 1937, Earhart and Noonan took off from Lae. Their intended destination was Howland Island, a tiny piece of land a few miles long, 20 feet high and 2,566 miles away. Their last positive position report and sighting were over the Nukumanu Islands, about 800 miles into the flight.

A coordinated search by the Navy and Coast Guard was organized, however no physical evidence of the flyers or their plane was ever found. Modern analysis indicates that after passing the Nukumanu Islands, Earhart began to veer off course, unwittingly heading for a point about 100 miles NNW of Howland. Researches generally believe that the plane ran out of fuel, and that Earhart and Noonan perished at sea.

Amelia Earhart goes down in history as one of the most courageous women who ever lived. Her accomplishments were incredible in the aviation world, which was still relatively knew and uncharted. She once said,

"Courage is the price that life exacts for granting peace with yourself." Without courage you will never move forward with your dreams and that fear will always get in the way. When this happens you will always be wondering "what if." What if I would have taken the risk, what if I would have tried, what if I would have not given up?

Although Amelia Earhart accomplished what many thought to be impossible, there was a failure. In her attempt to circle the globe on a 29,000 mile journey, she failed. Either by a mistake on her side or engine failure they came up short in their journey. Earhart once told her husband, George Putnam, "Women must try to do things as men have tried. When they fail, their failure must be but a challenge." She tells us to learn when others fail. So what can we learn from her? Among many wonderful attributes that this woman possessed the one that outshines them all is courage. Amelia Earhart was a woman of courage.

> Courage is resistance to fear, mastery of fear – not absence of fear

WHAT IS COURAGE?

The word courage derives from an Old French word "corage" meaning "heart and spirit." Some of the definitions for courage include:

- The state of quality of mind or spirit that enables one to face danger or fear with self-possession and resolution.

- A mental or moral strength to face danger with fear; bravery over an extended period.

- The quality of mind or spirit that enables one to face difficulty, danger, or pain.

Courage has been the agent for many of our successes throughout history. It was courage that led President Kennedy to make a statement that we would have a man on the moon by the end of the decade. It was courage for the astronauts to board the capsule that launched them into history. No one was 100% certain what would happen. We had never been there before. But in spite of fear the American team moved forward, and in 1969, America put a man on the moon.

THE FACTS ABOUT COURAGE

1) Courage is not the absence of fear

Courage is not living without fear, it is moving forward in spite of your fear. It is deciding that fear will not have the final word in your life. How many accomplishments would have never been achieved if we allowed fear to rule over courage? Mark Twain said it this way, "Courage is resistance to fear, mastery of fear – not absence of fear."

Don't decide that you will only move forward when fear has been removed, if that is how you think, you will never get anywhere. I am confident that Amelia Earhart had her share of fears. It's not wrong to have fear, it is only wrong to let fear control your actions.

I remember a time in my organization where I was embarking on a project that needed a significant amount of financial backing. I had lined up the necessary arrangements and began to move forward. One night it hit me, "If this goes sour, then I am the one who is responsible." I began to worry and fear was setting in. For the next several nights I would toss and turn thinking about the project. I started wondering, "should I back out, what if it doesn't work, what if everything goes wrong."

Fear was getting a hold on me and I needed to make a decision. Will I let fear control my future or will I stand with courage and move forward? I made the right choice. I would have missed out on so much and so would thousands of other people. Just remember that the courage you have to move forward will never be free of fear. Fear will always be there, but move anyway. As the famous reporter Dan Rather once said, "Courage is being afraid but going on anyhow."

2) Courage is based on belief and principle

Courage is easier when you decide your belief and principles upfront and then stick with them. That is what courage is based on. It is the values you have set for your life. You have made up your mind in advance and now you are making decisions based on those values.

For instance, if you are at work and some of your colleagues are talking about a business venture that has an outrageous return on your investment. The problem is that it is unethical. If you say, "you do not want in" then maybe you will become the outcast. What do you do? This situation is obviously going to take courage.

In the June 21, 1999, edition of Fortune magazine, the cover article titled "Why CEO's Fail," concluded that the CEO's were fired for a failure to execute or because they had lost the faith and trust in their people and then their boards. The common failing that drove all of this was "a lack of emotional strength." In other words, a failure of nerve and a lack of courage was why they ultimately failed.

> Courage is fuel that keeps you going when others would want to quit.

Maybe these CEO's couldn't make the tough decisions because they were afraid. Their courage was diminished because they never really set in place beliefs and principles that they could follow. When faced with difficult situations, fear wins, because courage has no backbone without a core set of values.

3) Courage is the quality that makes everything else possible

If you have dreams or goals for your personal life or organization you need courage to make them happen. If you desire great relationships then you need courage for the difficult times that relationships can sometimes bring. If you are an investor then you need courage when facing a risk that seems bigger than any other before. If you are a person of faith, you need courage to live it out when others around you are not.

In the words of Aristotle, "courage is the first of human qualities because it is the quality which guarantees the others." No matter what you're trying to achieve or what area of your life you want to grow you will always need courage to get there. Courage is fuel that keeps you going when others would want to quit.

Our hero in this chapter, Amelia Earhart, exemplifies courage. Every record she broke, every challenge she faced and every risk she took needed courage. Courage made everything else possible.

5) Courage can be lonely

Acting in courage can often leave you lonely. Sometimes you are the only one that has enough courage to stand. You may be the only one that has the courage to see the project through. Courage can leave you lonely in your business, career and even among friends.

Do you remember the sight of the lone Chinese civilian in early June, 1989, who stood unarmed, in front of a column of government tanks, blocking their advance? The famous photo was placed on the front of magazines around the world. I can still see it in my mind. The physical and moral courage of one individual could not be illustrated more graphically. The image fills us with both fear for his safety and pride in his action. He is the pictorial personification of courage and the world watched in awe.

He stood alone as you might do. Those who desire to reach the top and to live out their potential must choose a different path, the path of courage…there is no other way.

Building your courage and advancing professionally are similar to climbing a 6 foot ladder. The first step is low and wide and each consecutive step is higher and narrower. Near the top of the ladder, the ascent gets shakier as the steps taper. As you climb each step of the ladder, your motivation intensifies. Unfortunately, very few people ever make it past the first rung and only the great will ever make it to the top. The top can be lonely and fear is likely to set in, but courage is what it takes to get there.

Now you may never try to fly solo across the Atlantic or take the long 29,000 mile journey and circle the globe but you will need courage if you desire success in your personal and professional life. Here are a few areas where you may need to display courage:

AREAS WHERE COURAGE IS NEEDED

1) Ethical/Moral Courage

Tom was a young man who had a lot going for him at a young age. He was a former graduate of Harvard University and a recently selected VP of production for a nationally known pharmaceutical company. He had been married for three years and he and his beautiful bride were expecting their first child. They recently purchased a home in the suburbs and were moving forward to the life they had always dreamed of living.

At work Tom had implemented some of the business tactics he had learned and combined them with his own ideas and success was following. He had been there for about a year and was being embraced by his peers as well as his direct supervisors. One day Tom was brought into the office by the President of his department for a one on one conversation. In short, Tom was told, by the president that they were going to use a less expensive drug to produce their product. He was told that their clients were not to be told and to keep the conversation strictly confidential.

Tom went back to his office, shut the door and began to contemplate the conversation he just had. He thought to himself, "I am being asked, by my boss, to do something unethical. Do I do this or do I take a stand for my ethics?" If he stood for what was right he may lose his job and with a new baby on the way and a recently purchased home this could devastate his life. However, if he followed the direction of his supervisor he would destroy the very principles of ethics and morals that he has lived by all his life. Tom did make a decision. He told his boss that he would not be able to do what he had been asked and if that cost him his job then so be it. Tom was handed his final check and went home unemployed.

> Courage is the most important of all virtues.

Tom never regretted that day because he decided a long time ago, before he ever took that job that he would be a person of ethics and morals. Sometimes at work, or at home, you have to display the courage to stand for what is right; the courage to say that something is an injustice and you will not be a part of it, regardless of the cost. It is easy to stand for what's right when there is nothing on the line but it takes courage to take a stand when your livelihood is being threatened. When your future becomes uncertain then real courage will shine through. (By the way, Tom found a higher paying job 45 days later, and six months later his previous employers faced legal issues because of their immoral decisions.)

The famous poet and greeting card writer, Maya Angelou, once said, "Courage is the most important of all virtues, because you can't practice any other virtue consistently. You can practice any virtue erratically, but nothing consistently without courage." Real courage takes a stand when others take a seat. I value the writing of Robert Owen Stevenson regarding the courage to stand for the truth. This is what he writes:

THE ONLY WAY

The truth is but a simple thing,
for it knows no right or wrong.
There are those who would alter it,
to make the truth be gone.

They will speak, imply, suggest
what you know are not the facts.
But the truth will remain the same,
rest assured it will be back.

It may be for the moment,
the truth is not revealed.
There you stand betrayed by one,
accused of what's not real.

But for those of us who have been
wronged, take solace in what I say.
There will come a time where all will
know in some uncertain way.

The truth will rise above it all
and prove their words were wrong,
Causing those who spoke the words,
reputations now be gone.

The truth is but a simple thing,
it may be hard to say.
The truth is but a simple thing,
and for me the only way.

2) Personal courage

George Lucas once said, "You have to find something that you love enough to be able to take risks, jump over the hurdles, and break through the brick walls that are always going to be placed in front of you. If you don't have that kind of feeling for what it is you're doing, you'll stop at the first giant hurdle." Powerful words from a man who knows what it means to have personal courage.

His idea for the first Star Wars, in the early 70's, wasn't exactly embraced by producers throughout Hollywood. As a matter of fact, most people rejected the idea saying that it would not work. People said that America wasn't ready for something that seemed futuristic and prehistoric at the same time. Well, obviously, the producers were wrong. Star Wars has become the largest grossing series in history and has captured the hearts of people for nearly three decades. It was and is a giant success!

I once heard a quote by Mary Anne Radmacher that said, "Courage doesn't always roar. Sometimes courage is the little voice at the end of the day that says, 'I'll try again tomorrow.'" If you are someone with personal dreams and goals for your life you will need courage by your side. It doesn't mean that you will roar as loud as the next person, but it does mean you will keep pushing day after day, regardless of what you face because you know if you quit you will be left with unrealized dreams and a memory full of regrets. Jhoon Rhee once said, "Discipline weighs ounces but regret weighs tons."

Amelia Earhart must have felt this time and time again. Remember how she bought her first plane, but due to family problems, she had to sell it. She took a job as a social worker, but never abandoned her dreams. She continued to dream and envision herself flying until she saved enough money and started again. Dreams are wonderful things, but can become nightmares when we abandon them because they leave a lifetime of saying to ourselves over and over "what if".

> Sometimes courage is the little voice at the end of the day that says, 'I'll try again tomorrow

You may face times when the finances are not there to continue, then what will you do, quit or move forward? There are times when people will tell you to give up on your dreams. What will you do then? Will you stop dreaming or keep trying? Courage will need to be displayed at this time or you will find yourself dreaming from a distance but never living it up close.

3) Spiritual courage

This is a personal choice of mine to have a strong and active faith in

God. It is the most important thing to me, and it is the foundation for all success. Finances, relationships, career, dreams and goals are all stronger and more balanced under the umbrella of my faith.

This kind of choice takes courage. I remember when I was in high school and began to exercise my faith in God. One student, knowing where I stood, started to tease me for not being a part of their questionable activities. I remember him implying that it was a wimpy thing to have a faith in God. I will never forget my response to him when I said, "If you think it is that easy, you try it." He never said anything about it again.

Having a faith and living it out in your everyday life takes courage, especially when everyone else may be going in a different direction. However, it is the single greatest decision a person can make. If you have a faith in God, be willing to stand with courage. If you don't have an active faith in God then I encourage you to seek it out. It will be the best and most rewarding choice you ever make.

CLAIM YOUR COURAGE NOW

If courage has eluded you in the past, now is the time to demonstrate your heart and spirit and make a fresh new commitment to becoming a person of courage. Tell yourself that you are a person of courage; that nothing is going to stop you from living out the life you were meant to live. The past is done and yesterday ended this morning and today is a brand new day. Today you are a person of courage.

Claim your courage! Let it be seen in your personal dreams and goals. Let it be seen in your relationships. Let it shine through your career and your character. Let people all around you begin to see a brand new person who doesn't allow fear or insecurity to have the final word. Remember that you may be afraid at times, that is simply part of life, but move on with courage in spite of fear. In the words of World War I, Medal of Honor Winner, Edward Vernon Rickenbacker, "Courage is doing what you're afraid to do. There can be no courage unless you're scared." Live with courage or you will never really live at all.

Contemplate, Evaluate, Activate:

1. Is there an area or areas of your life where fear is holding you back? What are those areas?

_____

_____

_____

_____

_____

2. Do you demonstrate courage in your personal and business life?.

_____

_____

_____

_____

_____

3. Has there ever been a time when you have needed to stand alone in order to do what is right? What was the situation?

_____

_____

_____

_____

_____

Contemplate, Evaluate, Activate:

4. Has there ever been a time when you should have stood alone, and did not? What was the situation?

_____

_____

_____

_____

_____

5. What, potentially, is a lack of courage holding you back from?

_____

_____

_____

_____

_____

9

THE CHOICE OF VISION
Bill Gates

Over the past several years computers have taken the world by storm. Business people, parents, students and children are using them. We use them to store information, write letters, keep track of finances, design graphics and send information. They started out filling entire rooms, but now some can literally fit in the palm of your hand. And when you think of computers you most likely think of one individual, Bill Gates.

Bill was born on October 28, 1955, in Seattle, Washington. His father was a prominent attorney and his mother served on a variety of charitable boards. Skinny, shy and awkward, teenaged Bill Gates seemed an unlikely successor to his overachieving parents. While he showed enormous talent for math, young Bill, a middle child, was no one's idea of a natural leader, let alone a future billionaire who would reinvent American business.

Gates attended public elementary school, and then enrolled in the private Lakeside School at age 12. The following year Gates wrote his first computer program at a time when computers were still room-sized machines run by scientists in white coats. Soon afterwards, he and his friend Paul Allen wrote a scheduling program for the school. Still in high school, Gates and Allen founded a company called Traf-O-Data which analyzed city traffic data.

After high school, Gates set off for Harvard University, intending to become a lawyer like his father. Still shy and awkward, he rarely ventured out to parties unless dragged by his friend, Steve Ballmer, whom he later repaid by naming him president of Microsoft.

In December of 1974, Allen, who was working at Honeywell outside of Boston, showed Gates a Popular Mechanics cover featuring the Altair 8800, a $397 computer from M.I.T.S. which claimed that any hobbyist could build it. The only thing the computer lacked, besides a keyboard and monitor, was software. Gates and Allen contacted the head of M.I.T.S. and said they could provide a version of BASIC for the Altair.

After a successful demonstration at the company's Albuquerque headquarters, M.I.T.S. contracted with Gates and Allen for programming languages. The pair moved to New Mexico and started Micro-soft (they dropped the hyphen later). Although their new company's first five clients went bankrupt, the company kept moving forward, and in 1979 they moved to Seattle. The following year, IBM asked Gates to provide an operating system for its first personal computer. Gates purchased a system called QDOS (Quick and Dirty Operating System) for $50,000 from another company, changed the name to MS-DOS and licensed it to IBM. The

> It is the idea (vision) that unites people in the common effort, not the charisma of the leader.

IBM PC took the market by storm when it was introduced in 1981 and licensing fees streamed into Microsoft, ensuring the company's survival over the next several years.

Microsoft continued concentrating on the software market, adding consumer applications like Microsoft Word and Microsoft Excel. In 1986, when Microsoft went public, Gates became a paper billionaire at the age of 31. The following year, the company introduced its first version of Windows and by 1993 it was selling a million copies a month. When Windows 95 was introduced in August 1995, seven million copies were sold in the first six weeks alone.

With a reported fortune of $54 billion, Gates retained the top spot in 2001 Forbes magazine survey of the 400 wealthiest Americans. In 1994, he married Melinda French, a Microsoft employee, and they now reside in a 40,000 square foot home on Lake Washington. Taking after his mother,

Gates claims that he will give away the majority of his fortune through charitable contributions. His largest contribution came in August of 1999 when he donated $6 billion to his charitable foundation, the largest donation ever made by a living individual. Recently, it was reported that if Bill Gates wanted to spend his fortune in the next 40 years, he would have to spend $2.74 million every day. (I sure wish I could help him!)

Bill Gates is a man with vision and the entire world has benefited. "It is the idea (vision) that unites people in the common effort, not the charisma of the leader," writes Robert Greenleaf in The Leadership Crisis. These words could not be truer for Bill Gates. He is not a charismatic leader but his vision is big and people follow it.

I read once that he believed that every American would own a computer. It was a crazy thought years ago, but it seems so believable now. He said it in a time where people only reserved computers for large high dollar organizations; a time when most people had never even seen a computer. This was a big vision, something that many thought impossible to achieve. But now we find that many people don't just own one computer but two or three types of computers.

VISION IS A POWERFUL THING

He was a thirteen year old boy writing programs for his school who turned into a young adult taking risks that no one else would take all because he believed in his vision. Vision is a powerful thing. It makes a difference in people's personal and professional lives. Author and motivational speaker, Anthony Robbins once said "There is something magical about vision." When you have a vision for your life or a dream that you are working towards, it gives you a greater sense of purpose and a natural energy that is unexplainable.

Recently, Dr. Gail Matthews of Dominican University conducted a goal study. The study included 267 participants ages 23 to 72, from a wide variety of business organizations from around the world to study how goals are influenced by different actions. The Participants were divided into five groups.

Group 1 was asked to simply think about the business-related goals they hoped to accomplish within a four-week block and to rate each goal according to difficulty, importance, the extent to which they had the skills and resources to accomplish the goal, their commitment and motivation, and whether they had pursued the goal before (and, if so, their prior success).

Groups 2-5 were asked to write their goals and then rate them on the same dimensions as given to Group 1.

Group 3 was also asked to write action commitments for each goal.

Group 4 had to both write goals and action commitments and also share these commitments with a friend.

Group 5 went the furthest by doing all of the above plus sending a weekly progress report to a friend.

At the end of the study, the individuals in Group 1 only accomplished 43 percent of their stated goals. Those in Group 4 accomplished 64 percent of their stated goals, while those in Group 5 were the most successful, with an average 76 percent of their goals accomplished.

If you will take the time to consider the vision and dreams you have for your life or organization, work that vision out in your mind and on paper, you will begin to discover what Bill Gates has discovered for himself...vision works.

WHAT IS A VISION?

A vision is a guiding image of success. Just as a strategic plan is the "blueprint" for an organization's work, vision is the "artist's rendering" of the achievement of that plan. It is a description that conjures up a picture for you and for others to visualize the future. There is one universal rule of planning: You will never be greater than the vision that guides you. Just as an Olympic athlete's vision compels him/her forward day after day, year after year, so should the vision of an individual or organization stretch expectations, aspirations and performance. Without that powerful, attractive, valuable vision, why bother?

That is what vision is. It is simply a picture of how you see the future. It is a compelling portrait that inspires you and lights a fire in the heart of all who hear it. When you create a vision for your life or organization you propel yourself one giant step closer to turning that vision into reality.

WHAT VISION WILL DO FOR YOU

1) Compass – It serves to guide you

When you have a vision for your life, it serves as a compass. It guides you to where you are headed. Have you ever walked into a large mall looking for a certain store? If you cannot find that store, you look for a free standing sign that says "directory." When you locate the store on the map you look for a "star" or a "colored circle" that says, "You are here." You now know where you are and where you are headed. Then you figure out the quickest way to get there and your journey begins.

> You will never be greater than the vision that guides you

Vision is just like the map in the mall. You know where you are and your vision tells you where you are headed. Without the vision you don't know where you are headed because you never took time to map it out. So you become like many other people in this world "getting by" but never "getting ahead." You're like a person walking on a treadmill, lots of motion but no progress.

You might remember the actor George Sanders. He was a gifted man, a fine actor, musician, painter and writer. And yet he committed suicide. He left a note explaining the reason why. He simply said he was bored. He was bored because he didn't have anything he was trying to achieve. He was aiming at nothing. Vision gives us purpose. It gives us a target to aim at and a mission to accomplish. It is like an old lighthouse leading us from a dark sea of ordinary to a lit up world of what could be.

2) Clarity – It answers the question "what will success look like for me?"

A vision brings clarity by answering the question, "what will success look like for me?" If you had the ultimate successful life what would it look like? How do you ever know if you have reached success if you haven't drawn a picture of what it looks like for you? Vision clears up the confusion and brings clarity to the question, "what does success look like for me?"

Bill Gates knew what success looked like for him. It may have not looked like that for other people, but he knew what it meant for his life. He wanted to build computers that the common person could use, and he did it. His vision answered the question, "what will success look like for me?" That's what your vision must answer. It has to tell you in the greatest detail possible what you think your future will look like 5, 10 or 20 years from now. What are your finances like, or your relationships with family and friends? What will your home look like? What impact will you have on your community? That is the greatest thing about vision; it gives you a color portrait of your future.

3) Compels – It keeps you focused when everything around you is trying to blur your vision

Perhaps Henry Ford said it best, "Obstacles are those frightful things you see when you take your eyes off the goal." A vision helps you keep your eyes focused on the future when everything in the present is trying to pull you down. Like a propeller on a plane, vision lifts you up above the circumstance so that the eyes of your heart stay focused on the horizon.

> Vision clears up the confusion and brings clarity.

Imagine it is the Super Bowl, and two very talented teams have been battling it out for four grueling quarters. The offense and defense have given everything they could possibly give. With only one second on the clock, the team that is behind by only two points line up to kick a 39 yard field goal. The kicker lines up a few feet back from the holder and gets ready for the ball to be snapped. The opposing team and thousands of fans are jumping up and down attempting to distract the kicker. The cameras are focused in and millions of people are watching. He keeps his head down, trying to drown out the negative vibes that his surroundings are giving him. The ball is snapped, he kicks the ball and the field goal is good. His team has won the Super Bowl as a result of determination to focus on the vision and get the job done. If you stay focused on the vision it will help you drown out the noise of the negative.

A true vision has the ability to compel you to go when everything around you is distracting you or telling you to stop. The great legendary missionary David Livingstone said, "I will go anywhere as long as it's forward." The vision that moves forward compels you to keep moving. That is the beauty of having a deep seated vision. It becomes a source of strength when you are feeling weak, because you are not looking at what is. You are looking at what could be.

4) Captures – It takes a hold of other's hearts and won't let go

John F. Kennedy did not live to see the achievement of his vision for NASA, but he set it in motion when he said, "By the end of the decade, we will put a man on the moon." That night, when the moon came out, American's could look out the window and imagine the possibilities. When it came time to appropriate the enormous funds necessary to accomplish this vision, Congress did not hesitate. Why? Because this vision spoke powerfully to values Americans held dear: America as a pioneer and America as a world leader. The vision that had been cast by the late President captured American leaders and they were ready to respond. Risks were taken, work was done, the unknown was explored, finances were spent all because one man dared to make a statement saturated with vision and it captured the hearts of millions.

> Obstacles are those frightful things you see when you take your eyes off the goal.

The great former quarterback, Joe Namath once said, "To be a leader, you have to make people want to follow you and nobody wants to follow someone who doesn't know where he is going." A compelling vision gives those around you something to rally behind. It gives both you and those around you a great sense of purpose and direction.

We now know four things that vision provides you.

1) It is a compass for your life, guiding you down a path of possibilities.

2) It gives clarity because it answers the question, "what does success look like for me?"

3) It compels you to keep moving forward.

4) It captures the hearts of others.

CREATING A PLAN FOR YOUR VISION

Now that we know what vision can do for us, how do we create it for our lives? Many people have dreams. As a matter of fact, I would say that everyone on this earth has some sort of dream. It could be for their finances, career or future. It could be for their personal life, marriage or family. Whatever the dream is, understand this, we all have them, but very few live them out. So what can you do to live out your dreams? How can you turn your dreams into a clear vision with a strategic plan that will turn your quiet dreams into a loud reality?

> To be a leader, you have to make people want to follow you.

I shared in my previous book, In Search of Higher Ground, the process to fulfilling your dream or visions for your life. Let me take a moment to share an abbreviated version with you now:

Step 1 – Dream without reservation

In other words don't be afraid to dream! Dreams are wonderful. They are a canvass of potential in which all that is possible is laid out for you to envision. Dale Galloway, in his book Leading with Vision wrote, "If you don't have a few people laughing at your dreams, it may just mean your not dreaming big enough."

Step 2 - Put your dreams/vision in writing

I don't know what it is about putting your dreams and vision in writing but it just seems to help. Less than 5% of people ever put their dream on paper. So why don't you become one of the top 5% of all people and write out your dreams. When you write it out, keep in mind to be specific. By being specific it helps you set up an indicator that lets you know when you have reached the dream.

Step 3 – Make a plan for your dream/vision

I read once that "planning without action is futile, action without planning is fatal." It is vitally important for you to put plans to your dreams. For instance, if your plan was to receive a college degree, but because of work and family responsibilities it seems impossible, then write out a plan on how you can fulfill the dream. What kind of money will you need and how will you get it? How long will it take? How many courses will you be taking each semester? Write out a plan, and then begin to work your plan.

Step 4 – Be committed to do whatever it takes

Many individuals are great at starting things but they fail to finish them. When it gets too difficult they simply quit, leaving their dream exactly the way it was...just a dream. If you give up at the first sign of difficulty you will never make it. Have the courage to hang in there and tough it out.

CREATING A VISION FOR YOUR LIFE

There is one more thing that is important to remember when it comes to the subject of vision. In addition to having a clear process to fulfill each dream or vision, you also should have a clear vision statement for your life. I am not talking about a specific dream or goal, but a vision statement that describes what you want your life to become. A vision statement is a colorful description of what your life is moving towards. It is a guiding image of success.

> If you don't have a few people laughing at your dreams, it may just mean your not dreaming big enough

In 1939, Bill Hewlett and Dave Packard started a business in a garage they named Hewlett Packard. The two men created a vision statement of what they wanted their "garage business" to become. They called it the HP Way and it read, "a core ideology that includes a deep respect for the individual, a dedication to affordable and reliability, a commitment to community responsibility and a view that the company exists to make technical contributions for the advancement and welfare of humanity."

Obviously, this is a vision statement for their business, but I want you to notice that they spoke of a company that didn't exist. They stated what they wanted it to become and what it would look like. They used colorful descriptions such as, "ideology, deep respect, dedication, reliability, community responsibility, contributions, advancement and welfare of humanity." They spoke of what they were working toward their business becoming.

Your next step in choosing to have vision is to create a statement that would describe what you want your life to become, a colorful, lively statement that captures success for you.

Here are a few things to help you create your own personal vision statement:

1) Make a list of what you value

This is the first step in creating a vision statement, because your values will drive what your life will become. Values may include: family, honesty, faith, marriage, children, love, integrity, excellence, trust, joy, finances, teamwork, commitment, loyalty, attitude, etc. So make your own list of what you value, don't be afraid to list 10, 20 or even 30 things. After you have exhausted your ideas, narrow down the list to your top five and no more. These are the values that you cannot live without in your life.

2) Put the values in short phrases

Now that you have your top five values, begin to write out some phrases that would help you describe how you would want to live out those values. Make sure to include the value in the statement. For example:

Love – to love people with a pure heart… to love unconditionally… to show love through my words and actions.

Excellence – to strive for excellence in everything I do… to live a life of excellence

Integrity – live a life of integrity… to display integrity both privately and publicly.

Marriage – to have a rewarding marriage… to keep my marriage exciting and alive.

These are just a few examples of how you can take your values and begin to put it into short phrases that describe how you want to live out that value.

3) Put the phrases together for a rough draft

Next create a rough draft by putting the phrases together. You are not striving for perfection at this point; you are simply working at putting these short statements together in a very rough format. You might find that by combining a few statements you can successfully list your values in fewer words. Maybe if you combined some of the statements I listed above it would look like this:

"To show love in my words and actions to family, friends and those I don't even know." "To live with integrity and to be committed to excellence in every aspect of my life."

Note how we took the statements above and began to put them together. It is not perfect but it is a good rough draft to help you understand what it means to put your short phrases together.

4) Work it and re-work it until you feel comfortable with your new personal vision statement

Take your time and write out this vision over and over until you feel completely comfortable with your statement. Once you have arrived at your personal vision statement, put it away for a week or so and then re-visit it. Make sure that it still feels right to you.

If you will truly take the previous steps and create your own personal vision statement, you will be giant leaps ahead of many others who have still failed to create an image of success for themselves. The work will be worth it.

I have given you two different tasks in this chapter. First, writing out a plan to fulfill a vision or dream that has been placed in your heart. This is important if you want your dreams to take wings and fly. Secondly, I shared with you how to create something beyond a vision for a specific task, but a vision for your life and how you want it to be shaped. If you will apply these steps they will help you become a person of action, a person of vision, a person who is taking the journey to become great.

Contemplate, Evaluate, Activate:

1. Do you have a vision for your life?

_____

_____

2. Have you created a vision statement? If so write it here. If not take the time to do so. Then write it here, and share your vision statement with at least one other person.

_____

_____

_____

_____

_____

3. What are some things that tend to distract you from your vision?

_____

_____

_____

_____

_____

10

THE CHOICE OF EXCELLENCE
Walt Disney

It has been a household name for decades. Children and adults around the globe have enjoyed his artistry for nearly a century. Millions have visited his personal wonderland, and at some point have purchased souvenirs as a reminder of their visit to the "happiest place on earth." His unique brand of creativity and his pursuit for absolute excellence is displayed in every detail of his multiple, history making projects. The name is "Disney."

Born in Chicago, Illinois, on December 5, 1901, to Elias and Flora Disney, Walter Elias Disney has forever etched himself into history. Delivering papers at 3:30 a.m. every morning, to help the family, Walt understood the value of hard work. At a young age he showed a great love for the theater, and Walt would often study Charlie Chaplin movies to gain tips on performing. He attended McKinley High School where he began showing great promise as an artist drawing patriotic sketches for the school paper.

After High School he tried, unsuccessfully, to get a job as an artist at the Kansas City Star. Reports indicate that Walt had been fired from another newspaper because his supervisor said he lacked creativity. For the next few years Walt bounced around from job to job. Most of his employment was centered on the entertainment industry at places like Pesmen-Rubin Commercial Art Studio and Kansas City Film Ad Company. During this time Walt rented his family's garage for $5.00 per month and used it as a studio. He would stay up late at night working on animation.

He raised $15,000 from investors, quit his job and incorporated his tiny company called "Laugh-O-Gram Films." He made a deal to sell a series of fairy-tale cartoons for $11,100, accepting a down payment of $100. After six months of work, Walt's client claimed bankruptcy and he never saw another penny. Despite desperate efforts to make money, Walt couldn't pay the rent where he lived and moved into the Laugh-O-Gram office. His workers left him and he barely had enough money to feed himself. Walt obtained a client and received $500 for a dental hygiene film and poured those funds into a new effort he called "Alice's Wonderland."

With the few dollars he had, he purchased a train ticket to California and set up a tiny studio in his Uncle's garage. He wrote to a film distributor announcing that he was, "establishing a studio in Los Angeles for the purpose of producing a new and novel series of cartoons." The "novel series" was his half finished "Alice's Wonderland" cartoon. The distributor bought six Alice cartoons from Walt for $1,500 each.

Walt convinced his brother, Roy, to join him in California as a partner in his new business he called "Disney Brothers Studio." With $200 Roy had saved, $500 borrowed from his Uncle and $2,500 that his parents contributed (for which they mortgaged their home) the company that would ultimately change the face of entertainment began production in 1923.

When the Alice series was no longer in demand, Walt started to work on a new character that would be known as Mickey Mouse. "Mickey" was actually going to be called "Mortimer" at first, but Lilly (Walt's wife) didn't like it and suggested he call the character Mickey. Efforts to sell Mickey Mouse cartoons were initially discouraging, so Walt came up with a solution…synchronize one of the three cartoons to sound. "Steamboat Willie" changed the industry forever.

In 1934, production began on the world's first feature-length animated film "Snow White." Walt had convinced his team that the movie was a good idea by acting out the story and personally playing each of the characters. He worked on the film for nearly three years. One of Walt's animators worked several months on a 4 ½ minute sequence in which the Seven Dwarfs worked in the kitchen to make Snow White lunch. Although Walt thought the clip was funny, he felt it did not flow with the film and so it never made it to the final cut. This was the type of thing Walt had become famous for, making adjustments to projects at any cost, all for his pursuit of excellence.

"Snow White" opened at the Carthay Circle Theater in Los Angeles on December 21, 1937. The full length animated film generated enough money for Walt to begin building a new studio in Burbank. During the construction of his new building, Walt moved ahead on three more feature films: Pinocchio, Fantasia and Bambi.

Although his animated features were profitable, Walt wanted to do something different. He sent a team to film in Alaska and they returned with endless footage of seals that seemed to enchant Walt. While others saw miles of boring seals, Walt saw gold and he added music, clever writing, a few jokes and solid editing and the water loving creatures were the stars of "Seal Island", Walt's first True-Life Adventure. From 1948-1960 Walt made 13 True-Life Adventures and won eight Academy Awards.

One Sunday afternoon in 1944, Walt was entertaining his girls by letting them ride the merry-go-round, nearly fifteen times. He was quietly sitting on a wooden bench wondering why no one had invented a clean, safe place where parents and children could enjoy themselves at the same time. There on that bench, in front of a merry-go-round, Walt began thinking about creating an amusement park that he would call "Disneyland."

After much research and investigation Walt moved forward with his new dream. After being rejected by over 450 lending institutions, taking money out on his life insurance, selling his vacation home in Palm Springs, Walt was finally ready to begin building his vision. After years of hard work and countless hours of planning, Disneyland opened to the public in 1955.

Disneyland has become an icon in American culture. People from all over the world visit this place that began as a dream on a wooden bench in the 1940's. It is the home of some of the greatest animated characters such as: Mickey Mouse, Donald Duck, Goofy, Snow White, Mary Poppins, Beauty and the Beast, Nemo, Aladdin and the list continues to grow year after year. Children that are fascinated by it grow up to be adults that love it.

After all these years, Disneyland has managed to maintain it's pursuit of excellence, even after the death of Walt Disney on December 15, 1966. It continues to be the dominating amusement park throughout the world. Go and visit any other amusement park and you will not find the same performance standards that you will find at Disneyland. The grounds are cleaner, the landscaping is manicured, the rides are better maintained and the productions are performed at a higher level. Walt's pursuit of excellence continues throughout the Disney empire and as usual, excellence has paid off.

Regarding excellence, the author, James Gardner once said, "Some people have greatness thrust upon them. Very few have excellence thrust upon them…they achieve it. They do not achieve it unwittingly by 'doing what comes naturally' and they don't stumble into it in the course of amusing themselves. All excellence involves discipline and tenacity of purpose."

Most often excellence is not something that you are naturally born with, like the ability to jump high or run fast. You develop excellence by having the discipline to keep doing the right things and the tenacity to keep doing them when others have stopped at some point because excellence seemed too hard to work for.

> Some people have greatness thrust upon them. Very few have excellence thrust upon them…they achieve it.

That is how Walt Disney started, sitting on a park bench and realizing that amusement parks had settled for good when better was possible. He dreamed of a place where children and adults could come and enjoy themselves in a safe and clean environment. It was that desire for excellence that makes the Disney amusement parks stand miles ahead of the rest. It did not come automatically, but once again the pursuit has paid off.

So if excellence is a quality of greatness why don't more people pursue it? Why aren't more companies, organizations and individuals paying the price of discipline to obtain excellence? Consider the following negative ways of thinking that keep people and organizations from pursuing excellence:

Wrong ways of thinking that keep us from excellence

1) It's too hard to obtain excellence

Many people simply don't want to work that hard. They figure that all that work won't pay off, and if it does, is it really worth it? I have some friend's whose parents own a few fast food restaurants. These restaurants have been very successful and have provided a wonderful lifestyle for the parents, children and grandchildren. In the past few years the father had begun to step away from the business and started letting his two sons run the restaurants.

The sons were making all the decisions. The purchase of food, the hiring and firing, the marketing strategies, the budgets, everything was slowly given to them. They took it upon themselves to figure out ways to cut cost. They looked at their cost in food, labor, compensations packages, insurances and any other place where they felt they could cut cost, save money and increase profits. One area they discovered was in the food category. They noticed they had been spending quite a bit more for cheese than other vendors were offering. Because their restaurants served Mexican food, cheese was served a lot on their menu.

Without their father's knowledge they located a supplier who would give them cheese at a lower price. As a result the prices fell but so did the customers. People began to notice a difference in the taste of the food. When the father discovered what had happened he took his sons aside and discussed the problem with them. He shared that he found this supplier after months of looking for only the best product. Although it was higher in price it was worth the cost and effort to provide excellence for their customers. In the end, the two sons switched back to the original supplier, and the customers returned. Excellence is hard work, but it is work well invested. If you think excellence is not worth the hard work, think again. It could mean the difference between ordinary and extraordinary for your life and business.

2) Why bother if I've been successful without it

This is a trap. There are some people who are naturally gifted and can experience a moderate level of success without excellence. They ride on their gifts and abilities that have taken them to where they are at in life. They may know excellence is worth the work but why bother when "I have been successful so far without it." There are some people who have had success handed to them and don't see the value of excellence. Excellence for them is a battle they don't need to fight.

Joe Theismann enjoyed an illustrious 12 year career as quarterback of the Washington Redskins. He led the team to two Super Bowl appearances – winning in 1983 and losing the following year.

When a leg injury forced him out of football in 1985, he was entrenched in the record books as Washington's all time leading passer. Still, the tail end of Theismann's career taught him a bitter lesson: "I got stagnant. I thought the team revolved around me. I should have known it was time to go when I didn't care whether a pass hit Art Monk in the 8 or in the 1 on his uniform. When we went back to the Super Bowl, my approach had changed. I was griping about the weather, my shoes, practice times, everything. Today, I wear two rings – the winner's ring from Super Bowl XVII and the loser's ring from Super Bowl XVIII. The difference in those two rings lies in applying oneself and not accepting anything but the best."

> Regardless of how successful you have been, excellence is the ingredient that will take you even higher.

Joe Thiesmann was a great quarterback and great player, but he fell into the trap that many people fall into today. "Why bother with excellence if I've been successful without it." If you think this way…STOP NOW. Regardless of how successful you have been, excellence is the ingredient that will take you even higher.

3) Excellence is not natural for me

It isn't natural for most people. You make a conscious choice to make excellence a lifestyle for you. We want to blame it on natural selection. "Some people are born with it and some people aren't." That is usually just an excuse to get you out of hard work. It makes a person feel better about the place they are in. While others pursue excellence in their job or life you can sit on the comfortable chair of complacency blaming the whole thing on your belief that, "excellence is easier for everyone else, but it's so hard for me."

Regardless of the person's gender, age, race or economical status, excellence is hard work. There may be a handful of people that naturally pursue excellence and a handful of people that it seems to be easier for, but make no mistake about it…excellence is hard work and most people have to work hard at it.

4) It takes too long

When Walt Disney opened "Disneyland" in 1955, things didn't exactly go as planned. Opening day was being broadcasted on a 90 minute live television program that was the most watched TV event up to that time. Twenty cameras posted around the park telecasted a vision of exciting attractions, heartfelt dedications and relaxed commentary from Art Linkletter, Robert Cummings and Ronald Reagan.

> Stop thinking that good is enough when better is possible.

But like so much on television, reality didn't quite live up to the illusion. In fact, the park wasn't really ready for prime time yet. On opening day rides were broken down, there were too few trash cans, lines were far too long, and not enough water fountains were operating. Also, thousands of counterfeit invitations had been distributed, and so the park was overloaded, while the roads leading to Disneyland were jammed with bumper-to-bumper cars filled with irate passengers.

Not exactly how Walt would have planned it. But that did not slow him down. He fixed the rides and added water fountains and trash cans. The road to excellence was a long one for Walt Disney as it may be for you as well. It doesn't happen overnight, but the effort is well worth it. For "Disney" the pursuit of excellence continues. They continue improving, striving to be better than they were the year before. That is the kind of commitment it takes to begin the journey towards excellence, but the benefits that come from that long road will always be worth it.

If you are guilty of having the wrong kind of thinking regarding excellence, then at all cost stop thinking that way. Excellence will be worth the pursuit. Dr. Wayne Dyer said it this way, "It's never crowded on the extra mile." Stop thinking that good is enough when better is possible. Greatness can be achieved as you move toward excellence. There is always room at the top for those willing to climb the mountain of excellence.

STEPS TO PURSUING EXCELLENCE

Excellence should be pursued in your personal and professional life. When dealing with your marriage, pursue excellence. When doing business, do it with excellence. When creating a presentation, present it with excellence. When interacting with customers, interact with excellence. When operating your finances, operate with excellence. Don't isolate excellence; pursue it throughout your life.

> Excellence, I can reach for; perfection is God's business.

Here are some steps you can take in your personal pursuit for excellence:

1) Create a healthy drive for excellence

English Author and playwright, William Somerset Maugham had this to say about excellence, "It's a very funny thing about life; if you refuse to accept anything but the best, you very often get it." Decide right now; even say it out loud, "From now on, I am a person of excellence." Don't let it be something you say or pursue passively. Pursue it with passion. Examine your life, both personally and professionally and discover where excellence is failing and then with all that lies deep inside of you begin to pursue excellence like never before.

I am not speaking of becoming an annoying perfectionist, where nothing is ever good enough for you. These kind of people are difficult to tolerate and nearly impossible to work with. Excellence is what you are pursing; the goal is not to become a difficult to deal with perfectionist. Perhaps the actor Michael J. Fox said it best when he said, "I am careful not to confuse excellence with perfection. Excellence, I can reach for; perfection is God's business."

2) Choose it everyday, even when the emotions aren't there

Have you ever signed up for a gym, bought some new work out clothes and were ready to get in shape. You knew everything was going to change.

Your exercise patterns, your eating habits, your entire life was about to receive an overhaul. You go the first day and love it. You go the second day, and you still love it. But after awhile, it becomes a struggle just to get up in the morning and soon you hit the snooze button so much you almost break your alarm clock.

Now you started off great, but then the hype and emotions wore off and you were left with fairly new workout clothes that will hardly get used again and a gym membership that you keep paying for because you keep saying, "one of these days I'll get back to the gym."

This might be a trap you fall into with excellence. You read this book and it motivates you to begin pursuing excellence in a whole new way. You begin to think about the areas you need to change at work. The policies that need redefining, the facility that needs attention and the staff who need to shape up or ship out. Or maybe you begin to think about your personal life and the areas that need changing. Maybe it is your health, marriage or finances. Regardless, you are excited about the pursuit of excellence and all that it will bring.

> It's a very funny thing about life; if you refuse to accept anything but the best, you very often get it.

This is great. Be excited and passionate about excellence. I encourage you, however, to let your pursuit of excellence go past emotions. Make it a choice to do it everyday whether you feel like it or not. If you base this decision on emotion it will be short lived and unprofitable. Make it more than just a choice; make it a new standard in your life. In short, your commitment must outlast your emotions.

3) Realize that you cannot be the best in everything you do

Henry Kissinger, in his book, The Whitehouse Years, tells of a Harvard professor who had given an assignment and now was collecting the papers. He handed them back the next day and at the bottom of one was written, "Is this the best you can do?" The student thought "no" and redid the paper. It was handed in again and received the same comment. This went on ten times, till finally the student said, "Yes, this is the best I can do." The professor replied, "Fine, now I'll read it."

The professor wasn't looking for an "A" paper; he was looking for a student that was doing the best he could possibly do. Excellence isn't about being the best at everything; it is about doing the best you can do. Records that are set, at some time get broken. No matter what you do, someone will come along and do it just as good, if not better.

> Your commitment must outlast your emotions.

That's why you have to understand that excellence is not about being the best, it is simply about doing your best. Take a moment to think about your life, personally and professionally. Are there areas that need to improve, things that you can do a lot better if you would just try? I'm sure the answer is yes. Then do it. That is what excellence is all about. It is not a destination you arrive at, it is a standard for your life that says, "I am going to do my absolute best."

4) Create processes that enable excellence

When you go to Disneyland you will notice that a large number of their employees are young. Those that are serving at the refreshment stands, those who are selling the tickets, those who are in the parades and those who are running the souvenir shops are often young. Yet even with younger people with less work experience Disneyland continues to deliver excellence year after year. Why? Because Disney has created a process that enables excellence.

Disney has a standard by which the employees agree to follow. When each member of the Disneyland staff adheres to that, then the organization accomplishes its goal for excellence. With thousands of employees you can imagine how important it is to create guidelines for individuals to follow that would ensure reliable results.

You can do the same for your life and organization. Put some systems in place that would enable excellence. Think through some policies and procedures for both your personal and professional life that would help you assure excellence throughout. What are some guidelines you could put into place that would consistently give you the best results possible? This will take some time to think through, but it will be worth it. It will help to make excellence more automatic for you and your organization.

5) Think backwards

This is often a technique used in goal setting, but it can be used as well when excellence is your goal. Start off with the goal in mind. Think about a specific area where you would like to work towards excellence. Once you think of that area then begin to identify what excellence would look like when you started to reach it in that area of your life or business. Once you have identified a clear goal then begin to work backward. Begin to think about the steps you will need to take to reach your ultimate goal. There may be some changes that need to take place, some shifting of people, policies that you may need to create or other policies that need to stop.

This process will work with any area of your life where you are deciding to pursue excellence. However, I would encourage you, to take one project at a time. Excellence is a characteristic of the great, but you must be wise enough to know that it will not change overnight. Look at one area of your life and begin to work on that. Once you feel that you are making progress, go to the next one. You will find that it becomes easier as you move along, especially when excellence becomes more than a goal; it becomes a way of life.

> Excellence is not about being the best, it is simply about doing your best.

The great NBA coach Pat Riley said, "Excellence is the gradual result of always striving to do better." It is a constant goal, a daily decision, a passion that you must fuel day in and day out. It is not something you can do for a season in your life. It is something that must become engrained into the fiber of your being.

Remember that you are destined for greatness. You are special, unique and no one else is like you. You don't have to settle for less than the best in any area of your life. Always keep in mind that this is a process not a one time event. It is a choice you make everyday of your life to continue becoming all that you were meant to be. Always remember that what makes the great, great is that they are willing to do what others don't.

Contemplate, Evaluate, Activate:

1. Are there areas in your life where you could better strive for excellence? If so, list them.

_____

_____

_____

_____

_____

2. Do you allow how you feel (emotions) to control your pursuit of excellence?

_____

_____

_____

_____

_____

3. In your own words define the difference between excellence and perfection.

_____

_____

_____

_____

_____

Contemplate, Evaluate, Activate:

1. Are you a perfectionist; do you expect perfection from yourself? From others?

_____

_____

_____

_____

_____

2. What are some things you can strategically place in your personal life or your organization that will help you achieve excellence?

_____

_____

_____

_____

_____

NOTES

The Choice of Confidence – Frank Colapinto

1. Rohn, Jim. "Building Your Network Marketing Business." Made For Success. 1 Jan. 2008. Web. 21 Sept. 2010. <http://www.jimrohn.com/index.php?main_page=product_info&cPath=9&products_id=1699&zenid=qf0v2knttfpruk2v4vh1btt0s7>.

The Choice of a Winning Attitude – Bill Porter

2. Maxwell, John C. Attitude 101. Nashville: Thomas Nelson, 2003

3. Frankl, Viktor. Man's Search for Meaning. New York: Pocket Books, 1997

4. Outbreak. Film. 1997. Warner Brothers.

5. Door to Door. Film. 2002. TNT.

6. A study conducted by Gary Hamel and CK Prahalad as told in "Failing Forward" by John Maxwell. Nashville: Thomas Nelson, 2000.

The Choice of Focus – Jesse Owens

1. Cram, Mark. "Jesse Owens 1913–1980." encylopedia.com. http://www.encyclopedia.com/doc/1G2-2870400058.html.

2. Axthlem, Pete. Newsweek 1936. Print.

3. Lynch, Fred. "Ties to Michael Jordan Still Remain in his Hometown of Willmington, N.C." Newsweek 23 June 1997: 50. Print.

4. Kersey, Cynthia. Unstoppable. Naperville, Ill.: Sourcebooks Inc., 1998.

5. Maxwell, John C. Self-Improvement 101. Nashville: Thomas Nelson, 2009.

The Choice of Personal Development – Sally Kristen Ride

1. Streep, Meryl, perf. Bridges of Madison County. Warner Bros, 1995. DVD-ROM.

The Choice of adding Value to Others – Howard Schultz

1. Kouzes, James, and Barry Posner. The Leadership Challenge. Hoboken, N.J.: Jossey-Bass, 1996.

2. Graft, Lyn, and Ingrid Vanderveldt, prod. Primetime, American Made. CNBC, 2006. CD-ROM. CD-ROM.

The Choice of Character – Coach John Wooden

1. Ziglar, Zig. Sucess for Dummies. New York: IDG Books Worldwide, 1998.

2. Kouzes, James, and Barry Posner. The Leadership Challenge. Hoboken, N.J.: Jossey-Bass, 1996.

3. Hawthorne, Nathaniel. The Scarlett Letter. 5th ed. New York: Bantam Classics, 1981

4. "Unknown." Executive Speechwriter Newsletter 12, no. 1 (n.d.)

The Choice of Thinking Big – Oprah Winfrey

1. Schwartz, David. The Magic of Thinking Big. 65th ed. NY: Fireside, 1987.

2. Trump, Donald. The Art of the Deal. NY: Time Warner Book Group, 1989.

3. King Jr., Martin L. The Autobiography of Martin Luther King, Jr.. Boston: Grand Central Publishing, 2001.

The Choice of Courage – Amelia Earhart

1. Long, Elgen M., and Marie K. Long. Earheart the Mystery Solved. NY: Simon and Schuster, 1999.

2. Charan, Ram, and Geoffrey Colvin. "Why CEOs Fail." Fortune, 21 June 1999 http://money.cnn.com/magazines/fortune/fortune_archive/1999/06/21/261696/index.htm.

3. Bigelow, Scott. "Maya Angelou Entertains A Large Crowd at UNCP." UNCP. http://www.uncp.edu/news/2002/maya_an-

gelou_2.htm.

4. Stevenson, Robert O. "The Only Way." seeking Excellence Publishing. www.robertstevenson.org/pdf/Truthfulness.pdf.

5. Radmacher, Mary A. Courage Doesn't Always Roar. San Francisco: Conari Press, 2009.

The Choice of Excellence – Walt Disney

1. Reader's Digest, January 1992

2. Dyer, Dr. Wayne. It's Never Crowded Along the Extra Mile. NY: Hay House, 2002.

3. Riley, Pat. The Winner Within: A Life Plan for Team Players. NY: Berkley Trade, 1994.

ABOUT THE AUTHOR:

Chris Sonksen has a magnetic, captivating and humorous style for motivating and inspiring all audiences. He has spoken to thousands of individuals both nationally and internationally and there is no doubt that, by applying his teachings, his audience will improve the quality of their lives!

His vigor and talent for energizing audiences everywhere has enabled him to teach along side such celebrated and motivational giants as Rudy Ruettiger (the man behind the Tri-Star motion Picture "Rudy"); Coach Bill Yoast (the man who's life inspired the Disney movie, "Remember the Titans"); Bill Hybels, Ed Young, and Erwin McManus.

Chris is the founder of Celera Church Strategy Group an organization with an unwavering commitment to raise the national average of church attendance, by equipping church leaders with the tools and guidance they need to reach their communities.

He is also the founder and Lead Pastor of South Hills Church. Under his leadership, South Hills has grown to become a multi-service, multi-site church, impacting the community of Corona, CA and the world.

Chris serves as a life coach to hundreds of leaders of all types through his Blog "Chris Sonksen's Church Growth and Leadership Blog". You can find Chris's blog at http://chrissonksen.wordpress.com.

Chris is also available to individuals and groups for comprehensive life coaching and/or consulting. He works with business leaders to make improvements in all aspects of their business or church, career, work-life, and help to improve employer/employee relationship and team dynamics, including:

- Improving their leadership skills and intra-personal skills
- Developing team leadership
- Learning effective time management and goal setting
- Creating a healthy and fluid working environment

Chris is a native Californian, born in Long Beach and currently resides in Corona with his wife, Laura and their two children, Grace and Aidan.

For information regarding products or services, contact:
Celera Church Strategy Group | 2585 S. Main Street, Corona CA 92882
951-734-4833 www.celeragroup.org | info@celera.org